AF413767

THE

GROWTH

CAPITAL

PLAYBOOK

THE GROWTH CAPITAL PLAYBOOK

HOW SMART FOUNDERS FIND THE RIGHT PARTNER, SCALE FAST, AND BUILD WHAT LASTS

RICK FORD

Forbes | Books

Published by Forbes Books, Charleston, South Carolina.
An imprint of Advantage Media Group.

Forbes Books is a registered trademark, and the Forbes Books colophon is a trademark of Forbes Media, LLC.

Printed in the United States of America.

10 9 8 7 6 5 4 3 2 1

ISBN: 979-8-88750-772-9 (Hardcover)
ISBN: 979-8-88750-773-6 (eBook)

Library of Congress Control Number: 2026900865.

Cover design by Lance Buckley.
Layout design by Ruthie Wood.

Since 1917, Forbes has remained steadfast in its mission to serve as the defining voice of entrepreneurial capitalism. Forbes Books, launched in 2016 through a partnership with Advantage Media, furthers that aim by helping business and thought leaders bring their stories, passion, and knowledge to the forefront in custom books. Opinions expressed by Forbes Books authors are their own. To be considered for publication, please visit **books.Forbes.com**.

04-07-2026 9:45

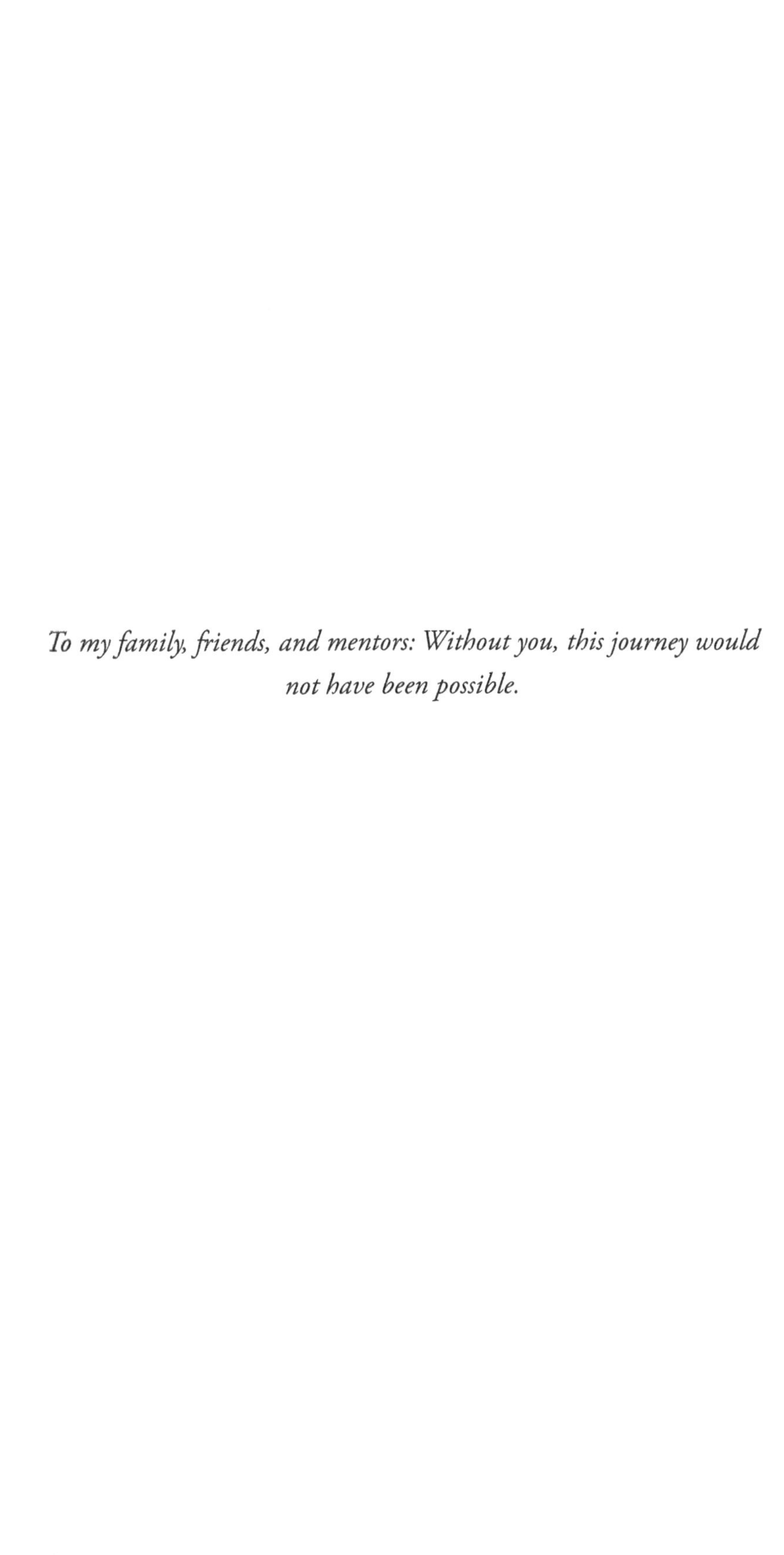

To my family, friends, and mentors: Without you, this journey would not have been possible.

CONTENTS

ACKNOWLEDGMENTS

I owe a tremendous debt of gratitude to the mentors, colleagues, friends, and family who have shaped my path, particularly Ted and Sheri Brewer, J. W. Ratliff, Buz Post, Randall Reed, Jeff Dyke, Mike Maroone, Brian Nerney, Eion Hu, Dan Williams, Myron Heronema, Tamara Bebb, Mrs. Jeanne Grubbs, Chris Ford, Chase Ford, Payton Shelton, and most of all, my wife, Brandi Ford.

ABOUT THE AUTHOR

RICK FORD is a seasoned entrepreneur, investor, and former CEO with over forty-five years of experience in automotive and capital-intensive industries. He is the author of *The Growth Capital Playbook*, a strategic guide for founders who want to scale their businesses through smart, founder-aligned capital partnerships.

In *The Growth Capital Playbook*, Ford shares insights from building RFJ Auto Partners into one of the top ten privately held dealership groups in the United States. Under his leadership, the company generated over $3.5 billion in revenue and delivered a 4.8-fold return to investors through its merger with Sonic Automotive in 2021.

Following the merger, Ford founded Ford Family Investments, a single-family office managing a portfolio that includes private equity funds, venture capital, joint ventures, and over fifteen direct company investments. His real estate holdings span more than 350,000 square feet across Texas, Oklahoma, Florida, and Montana.

Ford's mission is to help entrepreneurs understand that growth capital is not the enemy. It's a strategic tool when used wisely. He draws from his own experience to guide founders through the high-stakes world of equity investment while protecting their legacy.

He lives with his wife on Florida's Gulf Coast and maintains a five-hundred-acre ranch in East Texas. He is the proud father of three adult children and grandfather to four grandchildren.

INTRODUCTION

I didn't grow up thinking I'd one day run a multibillion-dollar company. I didn't have a road map or a degree from an Ivy League school. What I did have was a willingness to work, a curiosity about business, and a deep belief that if I kept showing up prepared and hungry to learn, someone would eventually give me a shot. I believed when that happened, I'd be ready.

My first job in the car business wasn't glamorous. I washed windshields and pumped gas from seven in the morning until six at night, six days a week. At the end of that first week, I was handed $120 in cash—I was too young to be on the payroll at that time. It was the most money I'd ever held in my hands, and in that moment, something clicked. I realized that effort could create opportunity. That if I kept pushing, I could go further than I'd ever imagined. That first job taught me the value of showing up and doing the work, no matter the task. And I've carried that mindset with me ever since.

Over time, I climbed the ladder. I went from service lanes to sales floors, then into management, and eventually leadership. I worked for public and private companies. I experienced market downturns, explosive growth cycles, and plenty of hard lessons. Along the way, I kept listening. I paid attention to people who were farther down the road than I was. I asked questions, studied financials, and watched how decisions were made at the top. The more I learned, the more I started to see a different kind of future—one I could build myself.

Eventually, I founded RFJ Auto Partners. We started with three people and a simple idea: Build something operationally excellent, rooted in strong values, and ready to scale. Over the years, that idea grew into a national platform with over two thousand employees and more than $3.5 billion in annual revenue. However, the real story wasn't just about the numbers. It was about the people who helped build it, the decisions we made along the way, and the lessons that shaped the outcome.

I've been fortunate to have had great mentors, people who shared their experiences and invested their time in helping me grow. They never asked for anything in return except that I pass it on when the time came. This book is my way of doing that. It's not a highlight reel. It's a look behind the curtain at what it really takes to scale a business, navigate partnerships, and build something that lasts.

If I can do it starting from a gas station in Texas, then so can you.

Why This Book? Why Now?

Over the years, I've had countless conversations with entrepreneurs who were asking the same types of questions. They'd grown their companies through grit and instinct. They'd built something real. But they were hitting a wall, either with capital, with talent, or with scale. They were hungry to grow but unsure what came next. For many of them, the term *private equity*, or, as I learned later, *growth capital*, felt like a closed door.

They'd ask how I built RFJ from a handful of people to a national business. How we brought in an equity partner, grew our footprint, and eventually merged with one of the largest public auto retailers in the country. More than anything, they wanted to understand how we made those decisions, how we kept our culture intact, and how we navigated growth without losing control of what made the company special.

There are thousands of small and midsize business owners out there sitting on something extraordinary who've proven their concept and built teams. But they've never taken on outside capital, oftentimes because they've never been shown how. They don't know what questions to ask or what a good deal looks like. They've heard the horror stories. They might worry about giving up control. Or maybe they wonder if they're even the kind of business growth equity would invest in. Because of that, they never engage with what might be the very thing that could take their business, and their people, to the next level.

This book is for *them*.

I want to take the mystery out of the process and reveal that capital is a tool, not a trap. When it's structured the right way, with the right partner, it can unlock growth you didn't know was possible. It can help you compete at a higher level, reach more customers, and build real generational value. However, you have to be ready and ask the right questions.

This is not a textbook but rather a lived experience. I'll share what worked, what I wish I had done differently, and the lessons that made all the difference. This book is about so much more than raising money. It's about scaling leadership, preparing for exits, and creating a business that still works when you step away. Whether you want to sell in five years, transition the business to your kids, or keep running it forever, my hope is that this book gives you the tools to do so with clarity and conviction.

If you've built something worth growing, then you're already on the right path. My goal is to help you take the next step with confidence.

How This Book Works

When we built RFJ, we didn't grow by accident. We followed a plan, adjusted along the way, and stayed committed to the fundamentals that had gotten us that far. The same approach applies here. This book is structured with intention. Each chapter is built around a clear theme, illustrated by the experiences, decisions, and lessons that shaped our journey from a three-person startup to a multibillion-dollar enterprise. The stories you'll read are personal, but the principles they represent are universal.

Every chapter begins with a central idea, one core belief or insight that shaped how we grew RFJ and how I continue to approach business through our family office today. From understanding capital as a growth tool to navigating partnerships, preparing for exits, and building infrastructure that endures, each chapter is designed to explore one critical piece of the broader entrepreneurial puzzle. These themes come straight from the trenches—real situations, real decisions, and real outcomes.

You'll notice that I often revisit the same key players, relationships, and values throughout the book. That's by design. Business doesn't unfold in perfectly distinct chapters. It moves in cycles. The same people who helped me throughout the early years of my career often reappeared years later during our growth years at RFJ and again after our merger and exit. The mentors who guided me early in my career became sounding boards for boardroom decisions decades down the road. The lessons I learned during setbacks often showed up again during moments of success. So rather than presenting everything as if it happened in isolation, this book embraces the layered, often circular nature of business growth.

You'll also see that I speak candidly about our wins and our mistakes. There were moments when we made the right call under pressure, and there were moments when we didn't. Both kinds of moments shaped our story. I believe that leadership means owning every part of the journey, not just the highlight reel. If you walk away with nothing else, I hope you carry this: Strong businesses are built on reflection, accountability, and the willingness to learn.

At the end of each chapter, you'll find a section called Timeless Takeaways. These are the core lessons that I believe apply across industries, business models, and economic cycles. Whether you're in your first year as a founder or preparing to scale into your second or third decade, these takeaways are meant to offer clarity and direction. They serve as quick reference points you can return to anytime the path forward feels unclear.

As you read, I encourage you to treat this book as both inspiration and instruction. Some chapters may feel directly relevant to where you are right now. Others may feel like a preview of challenges still to come. Either way, the intent is the same: to give you a real-world framework for thinking through growth, partnership, and purpose.

Business can feel isolating. Even when you're surrounded by a team, there are decisions that rest on your shoulders alone. This book was written to remind you that you are not the only one carrying those questions. I've been where you are. I've wrestled with the same doubts, navigated the same deals, and stared at the same ceiling at two in the morning wondering what comes next.

There's no single formula for success. But there are patterns, principles, and guideposts that can make the journey more manageable and more meaningful. My hope is that this book becomes one of those guideposts for you.

Let's begin.

DEFINING SUCCESS

*You can have everything in life you want
if you will just help enough other people get what they want.*

—ZIG ZIGLAR

When I think back to what success meant to me as a kid, it's almost laughable in its simplicity. At one point, success was saving up enough money to buy a bicycle. Later, it was scraping together $500 a month just to survive. I didn't grow up with a silver spoon in my mouth. If I'm honest, I grew up with a wooden spoon—one with splinters. I didn't come from money. I have often said I was the poorest kid in a poor town with only one stoplight. I came from grit. From figuring it out. From doing what needed to be done when there weren't any other options.

But the more life I've lived, and the more people I've had the privilege to lead, the more I've come to understand that success isn't a static concept. It's not about hitting a number and staying there. It's a moving target, always reshaping itself around what truly matters to you in a given season of your life. And if you're doing it right, that definition should evolve. Mine certainly did.

Early on, when I dropped out of college to start selling cars, my family was mortified. And frankly, I understood why. In the late seventies and early eighties, the car business didn't have the best reputation. There was a sense that dealerships weren't exactly temples of integrity. My decision to leave a potential career in medicine and head to a used car lot felt like a step down in the eyes of many people. But I didn't have the luxury of caring about optics. I had a baby on the way, rent to pay, and no financial safety net. I needed a job, not a dream.

And yet, looking back, that so-called step down turned out to be the first step forward into something far greater than I could have imagined. I found work at a dealership that sold Oldsmobiles, Mercedes, Porsches, and Audis—though in those days, Oldsmobile was the main draw. I started in used cars, which wasn't glamorous by any stretch, but it was there that I began to see the building blocks of a business I would later lead and scale.

Back then, we didn't have CRM software or marketing funnels. If you wanted repeat customers, you earned them the hard way. I kept a card file with every customer's birthday, their job, their kids' names. I'd send handwritten birthday cards. I'd call just to say hello. And you know what happened? They came back. They brought their friends, their parents, and their children. I wasn't just selling cars. I was building trust. And eventually, I realized that trust is the most valuable currency in any business.

As I moved up into the finance department, into sales management, and eventually into multistore leadership, the definition of success shifted again. Beyond taking care of customers myself, I was focused on creating a culture in which my team could take care of them even when I wasn't around. I was building something that could outlast *me*.

That's when the metric changed. Success stopped being personal and became generational.

I started asking myself different questions: How many people have I helped grow their careers? How many families have put food on the table because of the company we built? How many future leaders were shaped by the culture we created?

I never set out to be a CEO. I just wanted to be a good provider, a good teammate, a good boss. But somewhere along the way, those small, consistent efforts added up to something bigger. And now, when I look back, I measure my success not by my title or the size of the company we sold. Success for me is measured in people. The ones who started as porters, salespeople, or technicians and became general managers. The ones who once detailed cars and now run entire brands. Success is also seeing my three adult children become successful business leaders themselves, while at the same time becoming better parents than I ever was to them. They will take our family office well beyond what I have started and hopefully continue to grow it beyond my wildest dreams.

It all goes back to this lesson: Success is about how many lives you touch for the better. Everything else is just decoration.

Mentors, Models, and the First Dealership Lessons

Success didn't come to me in a lightning strike. It came in layers built over years, through hard days, long nights, and the guidance of people who were willing to take a chance on me. I didn't know at the time how lucky I was to have mentors such as Mike Hulsey, Jeanne

Grubbs, Buz Post, Randall Reed, Jeff Dyke, Mike Maroone, Brian Nerney, Eion Hu, and Dan Williams. Each one left a mark on how I see leadership, how I treat people, and how I run a business.

I still remember my first job in the automotive world, working at Mr. Ratliff's gas station, located in my small hometown of Kennedale, Texas. I was just thirteen. At that time, Kennedale only had one stoplight, and that gas station was right at the corner. My first task? Cleaning windshields and filling cars with gas.

Eventually, I worked my way up to changing oil, changing tires, and detailing cars. Mr. Ratliff demanded a consistent level of service for every customer who came to our station. Even back in those days, a full-service gas station was a dying breed, shortly before self-service became the norm. Mr. Ratliff required me to clean every window and check the oil, power steering fluid, and windshield washer fluid for every single car! Service was what we offered, and he expected me to deliver it to every customer every day! It was gritty, honest work, and it taught me a truth that's stuck with me ever since: If you want people to trust you, you've got to take care of every little detail. You take care of everything you touch. Mr. Ratliff was the first person to ever say those words to me out loud.

I was young, green, and nervous when I started at the Oldsmobile dealership, but that didn't stop Mike Hulsey from taking me under his wing. He looked me straight in the eye on my first day and said, "Rick, you don't know what you're doing—but that's OK. I'll teach you." And he did. What Mike taught me wasn't just product knowledge or how to close a deal. He taught me how to take care of people. He taught me that your real business isn't what you sell; it's how you treat every person who walks through that door.

I didn't realize it then, but that simple lesson was the seed of my personal philosophy on success: It's not about what you build; it's about whom you build it with … and *for*. Every day, he'd find a way to show me how leadership really worked through presence and connection.

We had a routine. After grabbing lunch at Wyatt's Cafeteria down at the mall, we'd walk the shops. Mike would shake hands, say hello, and check in with the managers and salespeople he knew. No agenda, no pressure. He wasn't working the room; he was building relationships. That's how he sold cars. One handshake, one conversation, one connection at a time.

> Real business isn't what you sell; it's how you treat every person who walks through that door.

That was my first real education in business development. I learned that selling is never just about the transaction; it's about trust. And trust doesn't scale unless you earn it consistently. Even then, I'd often take side jobs or help Mr. Ratliff with his old Thunderbirds that he loved to restore.

If Mike taught me how to take care of customers, Buz Post taught me how to take care of the business. Buz was a general sales manager at Moritz Cadillac when I met him, and although he could have led from behind a desk, he worked harder than anyone else. He was in early, stayed late, and only took one night a week off. When I got the opportunity to work at Moritz Cadillac, I was introduced to the power of metrics. They showed me how to break down the business by numbers—gross per unit, lead conversions, service cycle times. They taught me how to lead through measurement instead of gut feelings. The dealer taught all his managers how to understand a full P&L, not just focus on how many cars we sold. He often astounded me with his in-depth knowledge of the operations, gained not from his time walking around the dealership and observing but from analyzing the financial statements. But even with all that data, I never lost sight of the people. The dashboards were tools. The real work was in developing people who cared. People who showed up early, stayed late, and made sure customers felt seen. People like the ones who once mentored me.

When Buz got the opportunity to become a dealer, he took me with him, expecting the same work ethic from me that he demanded from himself. And I gave it to him. I worked from open to close most days. Sundays were the only guaranteed days off because of blue laws in Texas. I often ate peanut butter sandwiches at my desk. Sometimes, that was all I could afford. But I never complained. I knew I was building skills, instincts, and discipline. Buz taught me that leadership isn't about title or tenure. It's about showing up, doing the work, and being consistent.

When I moved on to work with Randall Reed, I met a whole different kind of leader. Randall ran on discipline. Up at four thirty in the morning, off to the gym, and at the dealership by six, he operated with intensity but also heart. We often ate lunch at his desk, talking through everything from P&L statements to store morale. Randall had a way of mixing excellence with empathy. He set up an employee fund so we could help team members going through tough times— quietly, with dignity. That kind of leadership sticks with people. It certainly stuck with me.

By that time, I'd worked in almost every department: sales, finance, parts, service, and reconditioning. I even handled janitorial work when it needed doing. That wasn't by accident. I believed, and still do, that if you want to lead a dealership, you've got to understand the pain points and possibilities of every single role. You've got to know how each department impacts the others.

Looking back, I can see how people such as Mr. Ratliff, Mike, Buz, and Randall shaped my perception about business and my work ethic. And in the chapters ahead, we'll meet several other mentors who taught me far more than any board meeting or investor call ever could. Through them, I learned how to be a professional before I ever had a title. I learned to take care of everything I touched (more on this in chapter 2), not because it was in a policy manual, but because it was the right thing to do. And I've tried to pass those lessons on every chance I get.

From Creed to Culture

Not long after we got RFJ Auto Partners off the ground, I realized something important: Growth wasn't going to be the hard part. What would be hard was keeping the culture intact as we grew, especially if we were serious about doing things the right way. I'd seen too many companies get big and lose their soul in the process. I wasn't interested in building that kind of business. I wanted to build something that felt as genuine at fifty stores as it did at one. That meant we had to be intentional from the start.

So I invited our early leadership team out to my ranch. We didn't go out there to talk about spreadsheets or expansion plans. We went out there to get real clarity on who we were, what we stood for, what we believed in, and what kind of company we were trying to build. It was one of those weekends I'll never forget. No distractions. No suits. Just a group of people sitting around a table, and sometimes a campfire, having honest conversations about our values.

We asked ourselves questions that went deeper than the typical mission statement fluff. What kind of people do we want to hire? How should we treat one another when things get hard? What kind of legacy do we want this company to leave? Out of those conversations came what I still believe are the foundational values of RFJ: honesty, trust, family, passion, and a drive to achieve.

We also landed on four core pillars that would guide every decision we made:

1. Employee satisfaction

2. Customer satisfaction

3. Market share

4. Profitability

In that order.

Now, I'm a business guy. I care about performance. But I was taught and have always believed that if you take care of your people first, the rest will follow. So I made that our blueprint.

That weekend, we created what we called the Creed Card. It was a small card, just a few lines long, but it held a lot of weight. On it were our core beliefs—simple, direct, and nonnegotiable. Things such as "We take care of everything we touch" and "We treat each other like family." Every employee got a Creed Card on day one. And they felt it. They saw it in how their leaders showed up. They felt it in how we handled adversity. That card became our compass.

Vision Statement

To provide value through innovative transportation solutions.

Mission

Our mission is to provide an impeccable experience by going the extra mile to exceed the expectations of our guests, associates, vendors, manufacturing partners, & shareholders. We will achieve this with integrity through commitment, innovative processes, & industry leading technology.

Values

Honesty & Integrity Doing the right thing in a trustworthy and sincere manner.
Trust Having confidence & belief in the honesty & reliability of others.
Family Having others' best interests at heart. Treating those you interact with as you would a family member.
Passion Possessing intense devotion & enthusiasm.
Achievement/Growth Motivated to the highest level of excellence by personal initiative, learning & development.

CSI Customer Satisfaction Index is measured by manufacturer data by brand.
ESI Employee Satisfaction Index will be measured by an annual survey and the benchmark standards will be based on published industry data.
Market Share New vehicle market share will be measured by our benchmark standard for manufacturer market data (minimum 100% effective) and sales effectiveness for like brands in the market.
Profitability Expected profit level according to dealership & departmental budget.

But here's the thing: Values don't mean much if they're only talked about in meetings or printed on break room walls. They have to show up in how you actually run the business. That's where a lot of companies fall short; they'll spend hours crafting the perfect mission statement and then go out and lead in a way that completely contradicts it. I wasn't going to let that happen at RFJ.

We made it our mission to operationalize those values. When we hired people, we looked for alignment. When we promoted leaders, we asked, Are they living the Creed? Do their people trust them? Are they the kind of leaders others want to follow? And when it came to performance reviews, we looked beyond profit. We looked at how people were taking care of their teams and their customers.

That's where the distinction came in between performing for profit and operating from purpose. It's easy to chase short-term results. It's a lot harder to build something that lasts. We were playing the long game. And that meant our leadership had to be anchored in purpose even when it wasn't the fastest or cheapest route.

> It's easy to chase short-term results. It's a lot harder to build something that lasts.

But here's what I found: When you operate from purpose, the profits come anyway. Our stores that had the strongest culture were almost always the top performers. They had the lowest turnover, the highest customer satisfaction, and the most loyal teams. Customers could feel the difference. And they kept coming back.

I'd hear stories all the time about a manager who helped an employee through a family emergency or a service advisor who went out of their way to take care of a customer on their day off. Those moments were evidence that the culture was working. That the Creed was alive in the business.

And the data backed it up. We tracked our employee retention and saw it far outpace the industry norm. Our customer satisfaction index scores kept climbing. We earned more referrals and built more lifetime customers than I'd ever seen at any company I'd worked for. Our people knew what we stood for. And they trusted us to stand by it.

To me, that's the power of culture. When it's baked into the way you lead, serve, and grow, it becomes your greatest competitive advantage.

That weekend at the ranch set the tone for everything that came next. It gave us a shared language, a clear standard, and a foundation we could build on, no matter how far we scaled.

Legacy Through Leadership

As RFJ grew, my role had to grow with it. I could no longer walk every store floor or greet every customer. I had to learn a different kind of leadership, one that could scale without losing the heart that made us who we were.

It's one thing to lead a team of ten. It's another thing entirely to lead thousands across dozens of stores in multiple states. The only way to do that is through people. Not just hiring them, but developing them. Not just managing them, but mentoring them. That's where the real work of leadership begins. It's not in the spreadsheets or the strategy decks. It's in how you invest in the people who will carry the culture forward when you're not in the room.

> It's in how you invest in the people who will carry the culture forward when you're not in the room.

I made it a point to stay close to our leaders. I held quarterly operating reviews where we didn't just talk about margins and metrics. We talked about people. We celebrated wins and surfaced concerns. We used those meetings to align on both performance and purpose. We also held town halls where I got the chance to speak directly to our teams, face-to-face, hand to hand. I told them where we came from. What we believed in. What we were building together.

And I listened. That was just as important as anything I had to say. Leadership, after all, is a conversation, not a broadcast.

But as much as I focused on communication, I also focused on clarity. Our leaders knew what the Creed was, but more importantly, they knew how to live it. We made that a condition of leader-

> Leadership, after all, is a conversation, not a broadcast.

ship. Taking care of your people was just as important, if not more important, than hitting your numbers.

I remember one store manager who pulled me aside after a town hall. He said, "Rick, I've never worked at a place where values actually affected how people got promoted. Until here." That moment stuck with me because that's how I knew the culture was real.

I also thought a lot about what Mike Maroone once told me. He said, "If you've been mentored, it's your job to mentor others. And when they succeed, they don't owe you anything—except to pay it forward." That became a core leadership expectation inside RFJ. Develop others. Coach them. Push them when they need it. Support them when they struggle. And when they rise, celebrate them.

Over my career, I've watched people rise through the ranks because they earned it. I've watched lot porters become general managers. Service techs become brand leaders. I've watched young people who once doubted themselves step into roles of real influence. And I'll tell you this: Nothing I've ever built, bought, or sold will ever match the pride I feel in those stories.

That's what success really is. It's not what you take with you. It's what you leave behind.

Yes, we built a business worth several hundred million dollars. Yes, we delivered strong returns. But the true return was in the people and the standard we set for what leadership could look like in this industry. That impact came from how we chose to show up—for our people, our customers, and our communities.

Because at the heart of it all was one principle: Take care of everything you touch.

TIMELESS TAKEAWAYS

1. As you are building your business, first make sure you and your leadership team are clear on what your culture is. Write it down, share it with all employees, and most of all, make sure you and every leader in the company execute on that culture every day. This will be important when you start the process of finding the correct capital partner.

2. Invest your time and effort into your people. Mentor, coach, and cheer them on. Start the process early and stay with it. The team you build will be the long-term success of your company, and *that* will add great value to your business as you speak with potential capital partners.

3. Remember to pay it forward. Always take great joy in helping your team grow, expecting only that they will do the same for others as they move forward.

WE TAKE CARE OF EVERYTHING WE TOUCH

It's the little details that are vital.
Little things make big things happen.

—JOHN WOODEN

When I say, "We take care of everything we touch," I'm not quoting a business slogan. I'm naming a standard I've lived by for over four decades. It's something that was handed down to me long before I put words to it. The mentors who shaped me didn't have a catchy phrase for it, but they modeled it every single day—in how they treated customers, how they showed up for their teams, and how they led under pressure.

When I was wiping down windshields at Mr. Ratliff's gas station, I was learning what it meant to have pride in every small task. If a windshield had a streak, I'd wipe it again. If someone pulled in needing directions, I gave them time and attention, even if there was a line. Mr. Ratliff didn't believe in shortcuts. Neither did my Uncle Ted, who was a role model for me and was the only father figure I ever had since I grew up without a father. They weren't flashy men, but they understood something about work ethic and dignity. You take care of what's in front of you, whether it's a windshield or a business or a person.

> You take care of what's in front of you, whether it's a windshield or a business or a person.

Later, when I started in the car business, Mike Hulsey didn't teach me how to sell cars by handing me a script or walking me through a close. He taught me how to treat people. He'd walk the lot with me, answer my questions, and make time for conversations that went beyond the transaction.

Mike showed me that leadership isn't about having all the answers. It's about making sure the people around you know they matter. That lesson sank in deep. Every time I walked a customer through a deal, I was thinking about more than the specs of a car or the size of the down payment. I was thinking about their family, their budget, their next chapter. That mindset turned into habits. I started keeping notes on my customers—birthdays, job promotions, anniversaries. Not because someone told me to. Because it felt like the right thing to do.

That's what I mean when I say we take care of everything we touch. We see the details. We stay present. We don't hand things off with half effort and hope nobody notices. Whether I was a porter cleaning a car or a finance manager closing a deal, I wanted our people to understand that care was part of the job. Not because we were trying to impress anyone, but because it was the right way to work.

Years later, when I became a general manager and eventually a partner, I carried that same standard forward. I'd walk the store and pick up trash in the parking lot if I saw it. Because if I expected others to care, I had to show what that looked like. When I sat in meetings, I listened with full attention. When we made a promise to a customer, we followed through. That principle—taking care of what's in front of you—became the thread that tied our culture together.

I didn't invent that idea. I inherited it and I lived it. And I refined it through thousands of interactions, setbacks, and small wins. It's easy to put words such as *excellence* or *integrity* on a wall. It's harder to show up every day and live them out when the stakes are high and no one's watching. I've found that when you commit to that level of consistency, people take notice. They lean in. They trust you more. They try harder. They care deeper. In business, that ripple effect becomes your greatest asset.

> It's easy to put words such as *excellence* or *integrity* on a wall. It's harder to show up every day and live them out when the stakes are high and no one's watching.

Somewhere along the way, I started saying that phrase out loud. "We take care of everything we touch." I'd use it in meetings, reviews, and onboarding sessions with new hires. Over time, it caught on, and it became a big part of how we operated daily. But long before it had a place on paper, it was written in how we worked.

What's interesting is how many people think culture comes from strategy, or maybe from branding. I disagree. I believe culture is built through behaviors that become habits, and habits that become identity. What we do, over and over again, becomes who we are. And what we tolerate, over and over again, becomes our standard. That's why I never let care become optional.

I've worked in places where people clock in, do the bare minimum, and wait for instructions. Those businesses rarely thrive for long. But when you lead with care, and expect it from the people around you, you unlock something bigger than productivity. You build pride. You build loyalty. You build a business that people want to be part of. That's where it all begins.

Taking care of everything you touch isn't about perfection. It's about ownership. If it crosses your desk, it matters. If your name's on it, you're responsible. If someone's counting on you, you show up. That's the standard I was handed by men who didn't have formal mission statements or company retreats. They had their word and their work. And they had people around them who noticed how they behaved.

I noticed, too. And I built my life around it.

Mission Is More than a Motto

There's a moment in every business when you realize the mission isn't something you write; it's something you live. It's easy to think principles are only tested in the big decisions—the million-dollar contracts, the growth capital deals, the hiring of senior executives. But the truth is, the integrity of a company shows up in how its people handle the forgotten corners of the business. How they respond when no one's watching. Whether a broken part is replaced without question. Whether a service advisor owns a miscommunication instead of blaming the tech. Whether the person answering the phone does so with warmth and clarity, even on their worst day.

> The integrity of a company shows up in how its people handle the forgotten corners of the business.

That's the part most people miss. Culture doesn't come from values printed on a poster. It comes from behavior that's repeated, reinforced, and respected. And if your people don't see you living it, they won't believe you mean it.

For me, that meant being willing to make decisions that cost us in the short term but protected our credibility over time. I can't count how many times I was faced with a situation where the easier move would've been to push something under the rug—to deny a claim, deflect blame, or squeeze out a little more profit. But those are the decisions that shape your legacy. We didn't build RFJ for the short term. We built it on doing right by people—our customers and, even more importantly, our team of two thousand associates.

There was a moment early in my leadership journey that's always stayed with me. A tech accidentally damaged a part on a customer's vehicle. It was a costly error. He could've blamed the condition of the part, written it off as wear and tear, or hoped the customer wouldn't notice. Instead, he walked straight into his manager's office, admitted the mistake, and asked to make it right. That moment told me more about our culture than any customer survey ever could.

But that kind of behavior doesn't happen by accident. It comes from leadership that reinforces the idea that doing the right thing isn't optional but expected. And most of all, it's modeled from the top.

That's why I always pushed my senior leaders to hold the same standard. I'd tell them, "Don't talk about the culture. *Show* it." It's easy to hand down values from a conference room. It's harder to live them in the middle of chaos. But when people see consistency, especially when the stakes are high, it builds something money can't buy: trust.

At scale, that's even harder. When we had forty stores across multiple states, I couldn't be in every meeting or on every call. So we developed systems to keep the culture alive. Town halls, weekly meetings, monthly operational reviews, and regular check-ins were reminders of who we were and what we stood for. Every leader in our company knew they were expected to carry the standard into their corner of the business—not just repeat it, but *live* it. And when someone fell short, we didn't ignore it. We addressed it head-on, because culture ignored is culture lost.

We also empowered our people to make the right calls without having to ask for permission. Everyone, from the sales floor to the service bay, had authority to a certain extent. If they believed doing the right thing meant replacing a part, waiving a fee, or correcting a billing issue, they didn't need to wait for approval. They just needed to be able to stand behind their decision. That level of autonomy can only exist in an environment where values are clear and trust runs deep.

Of course, there were mistakes. Not everyone got it right every time. But the goal wasn't perfection; it was clarity about who we were, what we valued, and how we treated people. When those things are clear, everything else falls into place. And when they aren't, no amount of strategy will save you.

People sometimes ask me how we built a company with that kind of consistency. The answer is simple but not easy: We said what we believed, then lived it, and then said it again. And again. And again.

That's what "We take care of everything we touch" really means. It means no one walks past a problem or ignores a detail. No one shrugs and says, "That's not my department." It means ownership at every level. Accountability from the front line to the boardroom. It means believing that the work in front of you matters, no matter how small.

The Real ROI—Developing People

There's a moment in every leader's journey when they look up and realize the scoreboard doesn't tell the full story. The revenue, the store count, and the EBITDA all matter, of course. But they don't move me the way they used to. What really moves me now is watching someone I hired twenty years ago run their own dealership. Seeing a young service tech rise into a director role. Watching someone who doubted themselves become the person others now look to for guidance. That's the real return.

I've always believed that leadership is about developing people, not just delivering results. That mindset came from working alongside mentors who made a habit of lifting people up, mentors such as Mr. Ratliff, Buz Post, Randall Reed, Mike Maroone, and Jeff Dyke.

Their habit of developing people rubbed off on me early. I remember being just a few years into my career, still figuring out how to manage departments and trying to juggle the day-to-day chaos of dealership life. And somewhere in there, it clicked: The people I was managing were watching me, for my decisions, yes, but also for my belief. They needed to know I believed in them before they'd ever believe in themselves. That changed how I approached everything.

From then on, I stopped thinking of myself as a boss and started seeing myself as a builder of people.

I can name dozens of men and women who came up through our ranks and are now running major operations. Some became dealers. Some now run public company divisions. Others launched businesses of their own. The point is, they left better than when they started with us. That, to me, is the best legacy a leader can leave.

But it doesn't happen by accident. You have to create an environment where people are expected to grow. And just as importantly, where they're *allowed to fail.* I never wanted a culture where people were afraid to raise their hand or try something new. That kind of fear kills creativity and initiative. I'd rather clean up the mess from someone's good-faith mistake than stifle their growth by playing it safe.

One of the ways we kept that growth mindset alive was by making people part of the process. Whether it was rolling out a new initiative, testing a tool, or adjusting a system, I wanted my teams to help shape it. People support a world they help create. When your team feels like they're building something with you instead of for you, they give it everything they've got.

It's also why I never believed in saving the good stuff for the executive suite. If you want to develop people, you've got to share the playbook. I was intentional about teaching my leaders how to read financial statements, how to think about strategy, how to evaluate acquisitions. I didn't hoard that knowledge. I opened the books, answered the questions, and treated them like future owners, not just current employees.

> When your team feels like they're building something with you instead of for you, they give it everything they've got.

Of course, that kind of development takes time. You can't microwave maturity. It takes reps and consistency. And it takes leaders who are willing to coach, not just correct.

I can still remember sitting across from a young manager, not much older than I was when I first got my shot. He was sharp, driven, full of ideas, but he lacked confidence. He'd second-guess himself, worry about making the wrong call. One day, after a tough conversation about a decision that hadn't gone well, I told him, "Listen, I don't expect you to never make a mistake. I expect you to own your decisions and learn fast. That's it." His whole posture changed. Sometimes, that's all someone needs: *belief.*

I've tried to give that same belief to as many people as I can, especially those coming up behind me. My kids, their friends, even folks in their forties just trying to find their way forward. And here's the truth most people miss: Developing people isn't just good leadership. *It's good business.* When your people grow, your business grows. When they feel seen, invested in, and trusted, they stick around. Not to mention, they protect the brand fiercely and solve problems before they even reach your desk.

That's the kind of return I've always been after. Because eventually, those people take the culture and carry it further than you ever could alone.

I've been fortunate to see that up close—people I once hired stepping into new chapters, taking the values we built, and spreading them into new corners of the industry. That's what I'm most proud of.

When people ask me what I hope to be remembered for, the answer is simple: He took care of people. And because of that, they became more than they thought they could be.

Scaling Values

It's one thing to take care of everything you touch when you can see it all from your office window. When you've only got one or two rooftops, it's manageable. You know the names, the stories, the birthdays. You can walk the floor and feel the pulse of the business. But when that business expands and stretches across eight states and more than forty rooftops, the real test begins. That's when values either scale or slip.

I knew early on that if we were going to grow, we had to be crystal clear about who we were and what we stood for. Because growth, as exciting as it is, comes with friction. It challenges the consistency of execution. You hire new people, bring on new markets, and suddenly your culture is being interpreted by people who weren't there when it was created. If you're not careful, the business grows faster than the values that hold it together.

> If you're not careful, the business grows faster than the values that hold it together.

That's why communication became nonnegotiable as we scaled. I didn't want to be the kind of leader who only showed up when there was a problem or a celebration. I wanted to be visible, accessible, and accountable. So we made town hall meetings a regular part of our rhythm. I'd go from store to store, not with a scripted agenda but with a willingness to listen. I wanted to hear from the team about what was working, what wasn't, and what they needed from us to do their jobs well. That two-way communication became a lifeline.

It also reminded me that while strategy can come from the top, execution happens at the store level. That's where the culture lives or dies. So we built systems to support our people, not just measure them. Quarterly business reviews were about creating alignment. We looked at the numbers together, asked questions, and shared feedback. Over time, those reviews became less about performance measurement and more about shared progress.

Still, scaling culture isn't about systems alone. It's about empowering people to make the right call, even when it's hard. I told every general manager, every department lead: You have the authority to do what's right by the customer. Period. If that means eating a repair cost, honoring a promise that wasn't documented, or taking a financial hit to uphold our standards, do it. I'll stand behind you.

That kind of trust takes time to build, and it only works when people see it in action. I can think of countless moments when our leaders took a short-term loss to protect long-term integrity. That's what creates loyalty internally *and* externally. People remember when a company does right by them, especially when it costs the company something.

Growth without care is just expansion. But when you scale with intention, rooted in who you are, and empower others to carry it forward, then growth becomes a multiplier.

The Mindset of a Builder

I've come to believe that thinking like an owner has little to do with a title and everything to do with how you approach responsibility. I operated inside businesses for years, long before I ever owned one, and it became clear to me that real ownership is a mindset. You don't have to hold equity to care deeply about outcomes, to make decisions with long-term consequences in mind, to weigh your choices as if the cost were coming out of your own pocket. That's what I tried to instill in our people. That's exactly the way I've tried to lead.

But here's the truth a lot of people don't say out loud: Ownership is not for everyone. In the same way that not everyone is wired to be a pilot or a surgeon or a performer on a stage, not everyone is built to be an entrepreneur. That's OK! Being an entrepreneur requires a unique relationship with uncertainty. It means being comfortable without a steady paycheck, pushing forward when no one is clapping, and making decisions without a playbook. You live with ambiguity, and you get used to solving problems without knowing exactly what's coming next.

When I started in the car business, we worked strictly on commission. No hourly wage. No base salary. You either sold a car or you didn't eat. That level of pressure could break you if you didn't have some internal engine pushing you forward. I learned early that discipline matters more than talent and that self-belief matters more than charisma. The people who lasted were the ones who could show up day in and day out, with no promise of reward, and still give their best.

> I learned early that discipline matters more than talent and that self-belief matters more than charisma.

Over time, I watched many of those same qualities show up again during those long seasons that test whether a person is really cut out for something. During the Gulf War and the oil shocks of the early 2000s, demand slowed, inventory tightened, and every decision felt like it had twice the weight. The financial crisis in 2008 hit hard as well, and there were nights I couldn't sleep, running numbers in my head and playing out worst-case scenarios. And then, of course, there was COVID-19. That was something else entirely, an almost surreal moment when the world stopped, and no one knew how long it would last or what would come back.

However, I never let any of those moments define the trajectory of the business. They were *part* of the story, not the whole story. Each cycle taught me something critical: You have to see the upside, even when you're planning for the downside. You can't allow fear to dictate your vision, but you also can't ignore the hard data. I've always been an optimist, but I've learned to be a cautious one. I try to think in layers: hopeful at the top, but grounded underneath.

Randall Reed was the mentor who helped shape that mindset. He believed we could sell our way out of anything. And more often than not, he was right. Randall had this incredible energy and drive, and he pushed me to think about what was possible, not just what was probable. To him, the market wasn't a barrier; it was an opportunity. He used to say that if we stayed focused on selling, we'd always find our way through. His philosophy built a kind of forward momentum that carried through our entire organization.

Working with the Moritz organization (which Buz Post was also a part of) taught me how to see the business through data. At Moritz, they were precise, methodical, and relentless about understanding the numbers, not just at the surface level but all the way down to the general ledger. It was with them that I truly began to understand how to dissect a P&L, how to measure profitability by department, how to identify patterns before they became problems. I stopped guessing and started forecasting. And I became a stronger leader because of it.

That balance between Randall's drive and Moritz's discipline became the model I followed. I knew we had to believe in the top line, but we also had to watch the bottom one. That meant learning the language of finance—getting fluent in things such as EBITDA, cash flow timing, balance sheet strength, and operating ratios. I didn't grow up in the finance world, so I had to study it the same way someone studies a foreign language. I had to look at enough financial statements, run enough models, and ask enough questions until the numbers started telling me a story. And over time, they did.

Later, as we began acquiring more stores, I took that discipline with me. I looked at over three hundred potential deals and executed more than sixty. I had analysts and advisors, but I never outsourced the decision-making. I needed to understand how each business worked, what its culture felt like, and where its real value lived. I believed that if I was going to put our name on something, I needed to stand behind it.

I want people reading this to understand that ownership, in whatever form it shows up, is about embracing responsibility. Whether you're an employee, a manager, or a founder, the mindset is the same. Show up with purpose. Learn every angle of the business. And when it's your turn to decide, do so with the full weight of the consequences in mind.

Culture, Capital, and the Cost of Compromise

As RFJ grew, one thing became clearer with each new acquisition: Taking care of everything we touch didn't just apply to customer service or internal relationships. It applied to the soul of the business. The companies we considered acquiring, the people we brought in, the partners we aligned with—all of them had to reflect that standard.

Culture became the first test we applied to any potential deal. Interestingly, the 240 deals we passed on taught me more than the ones we pursued. Some companies had great numbers. Some had solid reputations. But if the values didn't match ours, if there was a gap in how they treated people, in how they showed up for customers, in how they led their teams, we moved on. We could teach process or improve systems. But we couldn't rewire culture overnight, and I wasn't willing to compromise on what we believed in.

From day one, I stayed deeply involved in every single buy–sell. We never had a mergers and acquisitions (M&A) team. I reviewed every deal myself, not because I didn't trust others, but because I believed that vetting culture wasn't something you could outsource. Numbers can tell you a lot. But culture? You have to feel that in conversation. You have to ask hard questions, listen closely, and trust your instincts.

That approach came from the theme of this chapter: If we touch it, we're responsible for it. And that means we can't be casual about whom we partner with, whom we employ, or how we grow. Taking care of everything we touch means caring enough to be selective while recognizing that culture isn't an add-on.

That mindset extended to how we evaluated capital partners as well. Early on, I learned that not all money is good money. Too many founders make decisions based solely on valuation, but I've seen how damaging it can be when you invite capital into your business without alignment on values. Growth becomes transactional. Shortcuts get taken. And before long, you're running a company you don't recognize.

I was fortunate because the capital partner I chose respected the culture we wanted to build. They supported our vision and gave us room to lead. That kind of partnership made it possible to grow without compromising what mattered. But it didn't happen by accident. I made sure we aligned on principles—how we treated people, measured success, and made decisions.

Every time we considered an acquisition, I'd go through the same process. I'd write out the pros and cons. Not just operational details or potential ROI, but cultural observations. Who were the leaders? How did they talk about their people? How did they show up in tough conversations? Would they strengthen what we'd built, or would they dilute it?

And I never made those decisions in isolation. I brought my team into the process early because shared ownership always leads to better outcomes. Whether we were considering a new store or entering a new market, I wanted our leadership to see the big picture and weigh in. That collaboration helped us make smarter decisions. More importantly, it reinforced the belief that taking care of everything we touch starts internally with how we engage our own people.

Over time, we developed a strong internal radar for fit. If we walked into a store and something felt off, such as how the employees spoke to customers, how managers treated staff, or how accountability showed up in daily operations, we corrected course. We knew from experience that those early impressions often revealed the deeper truth. Culture doesn't hide well under pressure, and if you're not careful, it can unravel everything else you're trying to build.

> Culture doesn't hide well under pressure, and if you're not careful, it can unravel everything else you're trying to build.

I've walked away from deals that looked like easy wins on paper. I've passed on partnerships that would've given us fast capital or quick growth. But every time I said no for the right reasons, it made room for a better yes later. Protecting our culture was a long game, and it demanded discipline.

It also demanded clarity about what we stood for. Taking care of everything we touch meant honoring people, investing in relationships, and doing the right thing even when it wasn't the most profitable or convenient path. That philosophy extended into how we built our teams, how we integrated new acquisitions, and how we showed up in moments of uncertainty.

We didn't always get it right. Mistakes happened. But even in those moments, we used our values as a compass. And over time, that consistency built trust with our employees and partners, and most importantly, with the communities we served.

Looking back, I see that the deals I'm most proud of weren't just financially sound. They were culturally aligned. They helped us grow without compromising who we were and allowed us to take care of our people with a level of care and accountability that scaled far beyond the original vision.

When people ask me what made RFJ different, I tell them it was the standard we held ourselves to. When you touch something with integrity and clarity and heart, the returns take care of themselves.

TIMELESS TAKEAWAYS

1. Developing your people will drive your ROI exponentially. It is much easier to scale and maintain your culture throughout your expansion if you are developing your team, because they can help instill that same culture as you grow.

2. If you are adding a capital partner so you can grow your business, understand that, oftentimes, the single biggest deterrent to growth is not having people who already understand your culture and your values.

3. There are many paths to grow your business; however, most capital partners will look for growth in multiple ways, from organic to acquisitions to improved execution. Building a culture that is embedded throughout your organization will allow you to grow faster and more efficiently.

CHAPTER THREE

GROWING PAINS: WHEN CAPITAL BECOMES CRITICAL

Capital isn't scarce; vision is.

—SAM WALTON

I've always believed in hard work. It's how I was raised, how I built my first businesses, and how I managed to get RFJ off the ground in the early days. I didn't come from a background of inherited wealth or a network of financiers ready to write checks on my ambition. What I had was drive, grit, and a vision I could see as clearly as the Texas sky. I knew where I wanted to go. But at some point in every entrepreneur's journey, especially if they're aiming to build something that can scale well beyond a single location, they hit a moment of realization: Hustle alone won't get them there.

For me, that moment came early in RFJ's trajectory. I had bought one dealership. I could've pushed and pulled, leveraged every asset I had, and maybe, just maybe, I could've bought one more. But I wasn't trying to build a two-store operation. I had a bigger vision. And the truth hit me like a freight train: I could never build what I wanted to build without a capital partner.

That's a defining fork in the road for any entrepreneur. Up until that point, you're in the habit of figuring it all out on your own. You're bootstrapping, you're moving money around, you're solving problems with speed, creativity, and elbow grease. And that works … for a while. However, as you begin to scale, your business starts outgrowing your personal capacity to fund its future. And that's when the real question surfaces: Is this as far as I can take it on my own?

I meet with founders and owners all the time who are brilliant, passionate, and deeply committed to their companies. But they're stretched thin. Their growth has started to slow. Their working capital is tied up in receivables or inventory, and their infrastructure is lagging behind their ambition. They're stuck, not because their idea isn't good or their leadership isn't strong, but because they've reached the limits of self-funded scale. That's a dangerous place to be. And it's a lot more common than most people think.

Sometimes these people ask me, "Rick, how do you know when it's time to bring in outside capital?" My answer is usually this: When your growth potential exceeds your ability to fund it without compromising everything else. And when you're at that point, capital stops being a luxury and becomes a necessity.

There's a common misconception that equity capital is something you seek when you're failing. That if you bring in a partner, it's because you've run out of options. I think that's completely backward. Some of the strongest businesses I've seen, the ones with real momentum and traction, hit that inflection point sooner than expected. They're doing well, but they know they could be doing *better* with the right support. They're smart enough to see that capital isn't a rescue boat but a runway extension. It gives you the lift to take off further, faster, and more confidently.

In my case, that first leap into equity capital was less about desperation and more about vision. I didn't want to just own a few stores. I wanted to build a group, a platform that could scale, compete nationally, and attract the best

> Capital isn't a rescue boat but a runway extension. It gives you the lift to take off further, faster, and more confidently.

talent and best partners. But that kind of scale requires a foundation most people can't see from the outside.

That was when I started to realize something else: The hardest part about growing isn't always having the vision. It's funding the infrastructure behind the vision, essentially, making the dream *operational*.

This chapter is about those growing pains, the difference between surviving and scaling. That point when the friction between where you are and where you want to go becomes too much to ignore. That's when you start looking at external capital not as a crutch, but as a bridge.

Growth Planning Is Capital Planning

There's a moment that catches up with almost every entrepreneur. It's when you realize that your ideas are growing faster than your ability to fund them. That's the breaking point. It's not about creativity or ambition but cash. And more often than not, it happens because no one taught you how to build a proper capital plan. I know that because I lived it.

Early on, I was guilty of what I now see in so many entrepreneurs: I thought in terms of opportunity, not infrastructure. I saw the market potential, the customer demand, the white space. What I didn't think enough about were the facilities, the systems, the personnel, the technology stack—all the things that don't show up on a product pitch, but end up being the reason you can or can't grow. Capital planning wasn't even part of my vocabulary in those first stages. I was focused on the scoreboard, not the sidelines. But it turns out, the sidelines determine whether you even stay in the game.

Most business failures don't come from bad ideas, but from undercapitalization and poor cash flow discipline. Owners launch with passion, they find product–market fit, they hire a team, and then they hit a wall because they never planned for how to fund what comes next. They fail because they lack a fundamental understanding about capital, including *how much*, *when*, and *for what*.

> Most business failures don't come from bad ideas, but from undercapitalization and poor cash flow discipline.

If you think capital planning is just estimating startup costs and forecasting a few lean months, you're missing it. Growth introduces hidden costs that rarely show up in pitch decks. You open a new location, and suddenly your insurance premiums spike. You onboard a new sales team, and your IT system isn't ready for the load. You add a layer of management, and you realize you need new HR infrastructure just to support it. None of those things are optional. They are the costs of expansion, and if you haven't mapped them out, they'll find you, and usually at the worst possible time.

At RFJ, once we started growing at pace, I had to think far beyond the first check. I learned the hard way that for every dollar of revenue growth, you need to think about two things: the infrastructure required to sustain it and the contingency plan for when the environment shifts. Because eventually, it *always* shifts. The market turns. The supplier chain hiccups. A new compliance standard gets passed down. Suddenly, that growth you were chasing becomes the very thing that threatens your stability if you aren't prepared for it.

One of the biggest wake-up calls for me came during our early planning sessions, when we tried to project the capital we'd need to open our next few stores. On paper, the numbers looked reasonable. We had the cost of the land, the facility build, and the head count projections. But what we didn't initially factor in was everything that surrounded those moves—long-term working capital to carry the store while it matured, the training infrastructure for new teams, upgrades to our central systems so they could scale with the new volume. We had to learn to plan for launching the next initiative as well as *sustaining* it. That's a different level of thinking, and it doesn't come naturally to most founders. It sure didn't come naturally to me.

This is why I emphasize cash flow management as more than a financial discipline. It's a strategic one. You need to understand the rhythm of how it moves, where it goes, and when it hits friction. And most importantly, what kinds of pressure it can withstand when the business gets stretched. Because if you don't plan for that, the business will force you to. One way or another, you will feel it.

There's a saying I've repeated many times over the years: No battle plan survives first contact with the enemy. In business, I'd argue that no growth plan survives first contact with reality. That doesn't mean you just abandon planning. Instead, you now have a reason to do it better by building flexibility into your assumptions and leaving margin for the unknown. The best capital plans are resilient. They give you a foundation on which to adapt, to reforecast, to pivot without crumbling. And that's what protects you against chaos.

> In business, I'd argue that no growth plan survives first contact with reality.

Business courses spend so much time teaching entrepreneurs how to write a business plan. What they don't do nearly enough is teach them how to build a capital road map that matches the pace and complexity of real growth. One that accounts for not just what it costs to open a door but what it costs to keep that door open and make sure the next one doesn't bankrupt you.

If you're building a business with ambition, you need discipline. Because without that capital planning discipline, growth will expose your weaknesses faster than you can fix them.

Picking the Right Horse—and Being the Right Jockey

There's a metaphor I've used for years whenever I talk with other entrepreneurs about capital: Capital is just the horse—you're the jockey. And if you're trying to run the Kentucky Derby with a Clydesdale or a Thoroughbred with no rider, you're not going to get very far. The magic doesn't come from just having money. And it certainly doesn't come from just having ambition. The real performance happens when the horse and the jockey are perfectly matched, when the capital and the operator are built for the same race.

For a long time, I believed that if I just ran fast enough, sold enough, executed well enough, kept margins strong, I could ride any horse. However, the truth is, not every capital partner is a fit for every business. Some investors are built for steady cash flow businesses, some are chasing explosive growth, some want a fast turnaround and an exit. If your instincts and your plans as a founder don't align with the rhythm of the capital behind you, it creates friction fast. I've seen businesses fail not because the entrepreneur lacked talent, and not because the capital wasn't there, but because the two weren't running the same race.

When I started RFJ, I knew early on I wasn't going to be able to build what I envisioned without capital. I could've stayed small—bought a couple of stores, paid down debt, lived a very comfortable life. However, that wasn't the vision. I wasn't in it for the lifestyle. I wanted to build something scalable, sustainable, and ultimately transferable. And that meant I needed a horse with the legs to go the distance. But I also knew that the jockey, the operator, had to be worth betting on. And that meant I had to level up.

Equity capital can be transformative, but only when it's paired with the right kind of leadership. The investors I've worked with always look beyond the numbers to the operator. They ask themselves: *Can this person navigate complexity? Can they build culture? Can they handle volatility?* It's not enough to run one store well. They want to know: Can you lead when you're running twenty? Forty? Can you integrate multiple acquisitions? Can you scale systems, not just intuition? These are the kinds of questions growth equity partners ask when they're deciding whether to back a founder.

> Equity capital can be transformative, but only when it's paired with the right kind of leadership.

In our case, that meant building a dual-track growth engine: organic growth and acquisition. We wanted to do much more than sell more cars; we wanted to be able to buy the right stores, in the right markets, at the right time. And that takes more than capital. It takes discipline and operational maturity. It takes the ability to quickly assess whether a new acquisition is going to complement your existing platform or blow it up.

One of the biggest advantages equity partners bring is their pattern recognition. They've seen the movie before. They've watched integrations succeed and fail, and they know where the pitfalls are. But they're not in the saddle—*you are*. They're betting on your ability to ride, which translates to making sure your business can absorb growth without collapsing under its own weight. Planning not just how to buy a company but how to assimilate it for people, systems, culture … everything. The best jockeys know that winning a race comes down to steering, adjusting pace, and knowing when to surge and when to pull back.

At RFJ, we leaned heavily on both sides of the growth equation. We invested in building out a culture and an operational infrastructure that could handle scale, which allowed us to push further when the right acquisition opportunities came along. Our equity partners gave us the runway to think bigger, to move faster, but they also expected us to run smart. That required me to step into a different kind of leadership, one that could blend vision with execution, culture with capital discipline.

Never think the equity partner is there to save you. They're not there to run your business for you. What they're looking for is a jockey who understands the stakes, who's got command of the track, and who won't panic when the field gets crowded. If that's not how you see yourself, or if you're not willing to grow into that version of yourself, you're not ready for this kind of partnership.

That's why picking the right partner matters. One who is aligned with your goals, values, timeline, and style. You want a partner who understands your industry, respects your judgment, and is willing to run alongside you, not ahead of you. When you find that, and you're willing to grow into the kind of leader who can ride that horse to its full potential, that's when the game changes.

Know What You Want Before You Select a Partner

One of the biggest misconceptions I see among entrepreneurs looking for capital is this idea that getting a check is the finish line. The check is actually the starting gun. And unless you're crystal clear on what you're trying to build, who you're willing to build it with, and how you want to grow, that check can just as easily take your company off the rails as propel it forward.

It may sound trite, but partnering with a capital provider is like getting married. It's a relationship, not a transaction. And like any good marriage, it has to be built on shared values, trust, communication, and a vision for where you're headed together. If you're only thinking about capital in terms of access to money, you're missing the point and you're setting yourself up for pain and, oftentimes, failure.

Before I ever sat down with potential equity partners, I had to ask myself three critical questions. I encourage every founder I mentor to answer these for themselves, honestly and without spin.

First: *What am I really trying to accomplish?* Am I building a lifestyle business that gives me control, freedom, and steady cash flow? Or am I building something scalable, something I want to grow quickly and eventually exit? The answer to that question dictates everything that comes next. If you're in it for freedom and simplicity, you probably don't want an investor pushing for an exit in five years. But if you're gunning for scale, and you've got an eye on an eventual sale or IPO, then finding a partner aligned with that horizon becomes mission critical.

Second: *Do our timelines and growth expectations match?* Equity funds operate on a clock. If you're talking to a group that's already three or four years into a seven-year fund, they're going to be pushing for an exit much faster than you might be ready for. And that creates friction. One of the most common disconnects I see is when an entrepreneur assumes they'll control the pace, only to realize later that their partner is operating under a completely different timeline. You've got to surface those conversations early and be brutally honest about what kind of runway you need, how fast you want to grow, and what kind of exit (if any) you envision.

Third, and maybe most important: *Can we communicate honestly, consistently, and without ego?* That means being able to disagree without it turning into drama, being transparent when things go wrong, and being able to say "I don't know" or "I need help," knowing your partner is going to respond with support, not judgment. That kind of communication is absolutely essential. Because in business, especially one that's growing fast, something will go wrong. It's not an if; it's a when. And when it does, you want a partner who runs toward the problem with you, not someone who retreats into silence or blame.

In my experience, the cash infusion, or capital, a partner gives you is just the beginning of the benefits. What matters as much or more are the resources behind it: access to HR support, IT infrastructure, legal guidance, M&A expertise, tax and audit readiness, and, most importantly, people. When we had to scale fast, add new locations, upgrade systems, or manage a crisis, those behind-the-scenes resources made all the difference. You'd be surprised how many entrepreneurs take capital and then waste months or years building systems that the right partner could've handed them on day one.

But here's the catch: Not every firm fits every business. There's no universal best capital partner. There's only the best one *for you.*

But here's the catch: Not every firm fits every business. There's no universal best capital partner. There's only the best one *for you.* That's why I always tell people: Don't say yes to the first firm that offers you money. Fit matters more than check size. I've seen founders take deals with flashy terms only to end up locked into relationships that felt more like divorce court than a business partnership.

That's why you can't cut corners on your due diligence. You need to ask hard questions and meet the full team, not just the managing partner. Understand how they operate, how they think about value creation, and how involved they plan to be. Are they operators or financiers? Do they expect control, or are they looking to support your leadership? Will you be reporting to a board that rubber-stamps your decisions or one that second-guesses every move or, hopefully, an interactive board that partners with you?

What I've found is that true alignment is the only real foundation for scalable growth. You can't fake it, and you can't fix it later. If your vision doesn't match theirs, if your values are in conflict, or if your communication styles don't mesh, it will show up eventually … and usually at the worst possible time.

For RFJ, I was lucky. I found a partner who not only brought capital but also brought insight, operational know-how, and the kind of support you don't even know you'll need until the crisis hits. But it wasn't entirely luck. It was the result of years of relationship building, transparency, and mutual respect. We spent the time getting to know each other. We kept checking in, even after the deal closed. We operated like a team, one where we didn't just share wins but also shared the work and even the failures.

The Questions That Signal Readiness

One of the most common mistakes I see founders make is chasing capital before they are truly ready for it. They think of it like a badge to be earned, secured, and celebrated. But the truth is, capital is only useful if your business is ready to use it wisely. Otherwise, it magnifies the cracks, speeds up the chaos, and shines a spotlight on everything that isn't working.

That's why I always tell entrepreneurs: Don't chase capital. Prepare for it.

> That's why I always tell entrepreneurs: Don't chase capital. Prepare for it.

At Ford Family Investments, I meet with business owners every week. Some are early-stage founders with a lot of ambition and not much clarity. Others are operators with steady businesses that have reached a point of tension where they're trying to grow, but they're feeling the squeeze. More often than not, they come in with questions about money: How much capital should I raise? Should I take equity or debt? Do you think my company is ready for an investment?

The first thing I pay attention to isn't their pitch deck or their numbers. It's how they think. How well they understand their own business. Whether they're truly looking for a partner or just looking for a check.

I also take a hard look at where they're operating. Secondary markets often come with built-in challenges: limited talent pools, fewer institutional investors, and less infrastructure to support scaling. However, we saw those conditions as an opportunity. RFJ thrived in secondary markets because we understood them. That gave us an edge, and it taught me to look for founders who know how to turn constraints into strategy.

When someone sits down with me to talk about capital, I don't start with valuations. I start with questions. Ten of them, to be exact. They aren't written down on a form. They're embedded in our conversation. But they've become the lens through which I evaluate every opportunity. And if you're a business owner thinking about taking on a partner, I'd encourage you to ask yourself the same ones.

First: *What problem is this capital going to solve?* If you can't name it clearly, you're not ready. Capital should have a purpose. It should be tied to a defined need, such as expanding into a new market, launching a new product line, upgrading infrastructure, or acquiring another business. Too many founders raise money just because they can, without knowing what it's actually for.

Second: ***How much capital do you really need—and over what time frame?*** A rough guess isn't good enough. You need to understand your runway, your burn rate, and the impact of each dollar. I want to see founders who've stress-tested their models, who know what happens in best-case and worst-case scenarios, and who've mapped their capital needs against real milestones.

Third: ***Are you looking for a check or a partner?*** This is a critical distinction. A check gets you money. A partner helps you build. I've seen founders take capital from people who had no understanding of their business, no strategic alignment, and no interest in the long-term outcome. It never ends well.

Fourth: ***What does success look like for you, not just the investor?*** Some founders want to build a legacy business they can pass on to their kids. Others want to scale and exit. Neither is wrong. But if you can't articulate your vision of success, you're likely to end up on a path that doesn't fit.

Fifth: ***What's your timeline?*** This seems simple, but it's where most founder–partner misalignments begin. If you want to grow over the next ten years and your investor wants to exit in three, you're not on the same ride.

Sixth: ***How well do you understand your numbers?*** Not just the top line, but the mechanics underneath. Can you walk me through your margin structure? Do you know your fixed versus variable costs? Can you explain the drivers behind your EBITDA? If the answer is no, you're not ready for growth capital.

Seventh: *Have you built a team that can scale, or are you still trying to do everything yourself?* Capital is a multiplier, but it only works if there's a team in place to put it to work. If you're still holding every lever, your business isn't scalable. It is over-reliant on you.

Eighth: *What's your culture, and how do you protect it?* This is one that most people don't expect, but it matters deeply. I want to know what you believe in. I want to know how you lead. I want to know if your team would describe your values the same way you do. Because when growth accelerates, culture is either the glue or the crack.

Ninth: *What will you say no to?* Capital creates options. However, options, when unchecked, create a distraction. Founders who are clear on what they won't do are far more likely to build enduring companies than those who chase every shiny new opportunity.

Tenth: *Why now?* Timing is everything. Are you raising capital because you're in trouble or because you're ready to grow? The former is a rescue. The latter is a strategy.

These questions aren't designed to scare you but to prepare you. Because when the right capital meets the right operator at the right time, amazing things can happen. I've seen it, lived it, and watched it transform companies far beyond my own.

But I've also seen what happens when those elements don't align. When founders jump into partnerships without clarity and chase valuation instead of vision.

So here's the bottom line: Before you pick a partner, make sure you've done the harder work of understanding yourself. Know the race you're running. Know the kind of rider you are. And make sure your horse and your partner can go the distance with you.

Because in the end, capital doesn't build companies. People do.

TIMELESS TAKEAWAYS

1. Don't wait until the need for capital becomes urgent to figure out how you're going to raise it. Before you ever approach a potential investor, be able to clearly articulate three things: why you want the capital, where and how it will be deployed within your business, and when you'll need it. Investors want to know that you've thought this through, not just at a high level, but down to the details. Whether it's for acquisitions, operational expansion, technology, or infrastructure, be specific. Precision earns confidence. Vagueness raises red flags.

2. There's a big difference between wanting capital and being ready for it. Preparation doesn't just mean having a slick pitch deck. It means your house is in order: Your financials are clean, your legal structure is sound, your business model is well-defined, and your leadership team is aligned. A capital partner is not there to fix your foundation. They're there to help you build on it. Be honest with yourself. If someone wrote you a check tomorrow, could your organization put that money to work efficiently and responsibly? If not, focus on getting ready before you focus on raising capital.

3. The right capital partner is not just someone who has money but someone who understands your vision, shares your values, and brings the right kind of support. Take your time. Don't rush the process. Ask the hard questions, and more importantly, make sure they ask hard questions in return. That shows engagement, not opposition. Fit matters. Chemistry matters. Alignment matters. You are, in essence, getting married in a business sense, so don't settle for someone who looks good on paper but doesn't feel right in practice. The wrong partner can slow you down or pull you off course. The right one will help you scale further and faster than you could have on your own.

UNDERSTANDING THE "RIGHT" TYPE OF CAPITAL

If you don't know where you're going, any road will get you there.

—LEWIS CARROLL

In business, the people you choose to partner with matter as much as the business itself. I learned this early on from one of my earliest mentors, who warned me about the "sharp-elbow crowd." At the time, I wasn't quite sure what he meant. I figured it was just another colorful expression in the world of dealmaking. But the longer I've been in business, the more I've come to understand what he was talking about. There are capital partners who will champion your vision, walk beside you, and help you scale wisely. And then there are the ones who are all elbows—always nudging for more control, cutting corners, and pushing decisions that serve their spreadsheet instead of your people.

Most entrepreneurs, especially first-time founders, don't know there's a difference. They think capital is capital. Money is money. If someone wants to invest, it must be a good thing, right? That's the first trap. When you've been building something from scratch—scraping by, stretching payroll, trying to find just enough cash to cover your next opportunity—it's tempting to believe that the biggest check is the best one. But experience has taught me otherwise. Every dollar comes with a point of view. And if that point of view doesn't match yours, the relationship will break before the business does.

> Every dollar comes with a point of view. And if that point of view doesn't match yours, the relationship will break before the business does.

I've seen it happen too many times. Entrepreneurs who thought they were getting a partner ended up getting an overlord. Others who believed they were being rescued realized too late that they'd sold their autonomy. For those who didn't take the time to fully understand the personalities behind the capital, the cost was often far greater than they had imagined, both financially and personally.

What I've learned is this: Capital has a personality. It can be collaborative, patient, and strategic. Or it can be aggressive, transactional, and impatient. Just like people, capital shows its true character when things get hard. During the good times, everyone gets along. But when the numbers miss, or the market shifts, or a tough decision has to be made, that's when the elbows come out.

This is why I always tell founders to ask better questions before they sign anything. Don't just look at the offer sheet. Don't just calculate your take-home or focus on valuation. Ask yourself: *Who are these people? What's their track record? How do they behave when deals go sideways? Do they understand the industry, or are they chasing returns? Are they willing to invest in my leadership, or are they looking for a reason to replace me?* And maybe most importantly, *Do they treat people with respect when no one's watching?*

There was a time early in my own growth journey when we were entertaining interest from several firms. We'd grown fast, and our numbers looked good. What struck me during those early conversations wasn't just the size of the offers but how each firm viewed our people. Some asked about systems and metrics. Others went straight to cost cutting. A few never even mentioned our team. One group stood out. They asked about culture. They asked how we'd built loyalty. They asked how we trained new managers and how we made sure our values didn't erode across different stores. That's when I knew we were speaking the same language.

Too many capital relationships fall apart not because the numbers didn't work but because the people weren't aligned. That's the part no one tells you. The structure of the deal matters, of course, but structure is only as strong as the trust behind it. If you don't trust your partner, and if they don't trust you, it won't matter how well the documents are written. At some point, the relationship will fail.

I've also seen founders underestimate what happens when that trust is broken. Once you've brought a partner into your business, your decision-making no longer lives in a vacuum. You can't pivot without consensus. You can't ride out a bad quarter without explanation. And if your partner doesn't believe in your long-term vision, they'll start pushing for short-term wins. That's when things start to get uncomfortable. That's when the elbows come out. By then, it's often too late to reset the relationship.

So before you accept a check, before you agree to anything, ask yourself what kind of partner you're actually looking for. Do you want someone who will back your vision, even if it takes time? Do you want someone who sees the full picture, not just the P&L? Are you willing to have hard conversations early so you don't have harder ones later? Because I can tell you from experience, the easiest conversations happen on the front end. And the most expensive ones happen when you realize you chose the wrong partner for the wrong reasons.

The sharp-elbow crowd is out there. They're not always easy to spot. Some wear nice suits and say all the right things in the pitch meeting. But if you listen closely, you'll notice what they value and, more importantly, what they don't. My advice? Don't let the numbers blind you. Look for how they show up when it's time to roll up their sleeves. The right capital partner won't just fund your growth. They'll grow with you.

> The right capital partner won't just fund your growth. They'll grow with you.

Capital Comes in Many Flavors

One of the things I often tell entrepreneurs is this: Saying you want capital is like saying you want food. It's too vague to be helpful. Are you craving a steak? A salad? Something fast, something slow-cooked, something that fills you up or fuels you for later? The same applies to capital. If you don't know what you need and why you need it, you're going to end up with something that might look good on the plate but leaves you with indigestion.

Early on, I didn't know that. I thought capital was capital. You either got a loan from a bank or you raised money from someone with deeper pockets than you. I figured if someone wanted to put money into my business, that was a win. What I learned over time is that every type of capital comes with its own flavor, its own cost, and its own expectations. And you better understand those before you ever take the first bite.

Let's start at the beginning. The earliest form of capital, for most founders, comes from **friends and family**. It's not formal. There are no pitch decks or investor updates. It's your uncle, your college roommate, or someone who believes in you more than they understand your business. In chapter 6, we'll cover my experiences with these early forms of capital. But overall, the benefit here is *flexibility*. These are people who trust you. But that also comes with pressure. Because if things go sideways—and they often do—you're not just explaining the loss to an investor. You're sitting across the Thanksgiving table from someone who staked their savings on your dream.

Next up is the **angel investor**. These are typically high-net-worth individuals who are comfortable placing early bets. They know some of those bets won't pay off. But when they do, the returns can be significant. Angels can be helpful when you need more than your family can provide, but you're not yet ready for professional capital. The best angel investors bring more than a check. They bring *perspective*. And if they've walked the path before, they'll save you from a few landmines. Still, it's a relationship built on faith. You need to be honest about your progress and clear about your goals.

From there, the next tier is **venture capitalists (VCs)**. This is where things get more structured. VCs are managing other people's money, and that means accountability. It also means pressure to scale. Fast. They're not just betting on your product; they're betting on your ability to grow aggressively and find an exit. Whether that's through acquisition, a secondary sale, or, in rare cases, an IPO. VC money can be rocket fuel, but it's not for everyone. If you're not prepared to give up control, or you're building something that grows slowly and steadily, you're going to feel the mismatch early.

Then you have **family offices**. These vary widely, but they're generally more flexible than VCs and more patient than traditional private equity. Many of them are set up by wealthy families to manage their own capital across generations. They're not chasing a fund cycle. They don't need to exit in five years. But they *are* selective. A good family office partner will look at your values, your vision, and your leadership as much as your numbers. I've had several conversations with family office investors who asked more about my team than my forecasts. That tells you something.

And finally, there's **private equity (PE)**. This is the stage at which your business has proven results, steady cash flow, and room to scale. PE firms come in many varieties; some specialize in roll-ups, others in turnarounds. Some take a controlling stake, while others prefer to back strong operators. What they all have in common is discipline. They'll examine every detail of your business, from your financials to your vendor agreements to your leadership pipeline. It can feel intense. But the right PE partner can unlock growth you can't access on your own, provided you're aligned on direction and values.

Now, just as the types of capital vary, so do the structures. I've used everything from simple loans to convertible notes. A **convertible note** is a form of debt that can convert into equity under certain conditions, usually when a company raises its next round. It's a tool often used in early-stage financing when it's hard to set a valuation. But it's not limited to startups. I've used convertible notes in later-stage deals when we needed working capital quickly but wanted to wait to finalize terms.

Then you have **equity structures**. Some investors want a majority stake. That gives them control and decision-making authority. Others prefer a minority stake, allowing them to support without steering the ship. There are pros and cons to both. Majority investors can bring in resources and make fast decisions, but you may lose autonomy. Minority investors tend to be less intrusive, but they expect strong communication and consistent results.

It's not just about ownership. A smart capital partner brings more than money. They might offer support in HR, technology, legal, or operations. One of the best partnerships I ever had brought in a world-class CFO leader who transformed our financial discipline and reporting. She became a true partner for me and was a huge part of our success story. That wasn't in the pitch deck. It wasn't in the agreement. But it changed the game for us. These are the things that don't show up in the spreadsheet but make all the difference in the outcome.

That's why I go back to the food metaphor. You wouldn't walk into a restaurant and say, "Bring me food." You'd think about what you're hungry for, what your body needs, and what's going to help you feel your best. The same applies to capital.

Before you sit down at the table, figure out what you need. Is it flexibility or scale? Speed or staying power? A silent partner or a strategic one?

Because once you sign, you're committed.

You've made a choice. And just like a meal, if you chose wrong, you're the one who has to live with it.

> Before you sit down at the table, figure out what you need. Is it flexibility or scale? Speed or staying power? A silent partner or a strategic one? Because once you sign, you're committed.

One Size Doesn't Fit All

If there's one truth I've learned across industries, it's that capital is never a one-size-fits-all solution. What works in one business might completely wreck another. A capital structure that supercharges a SaaS company might choke the life out of a logistics business. And yet, too often, entrepreneurs chase after what worked for someone else, thinking they can cut and paste the strategy. They end up learning the hard way that alignment matters. The nature of your business dictates the nature of your capital.

Let me explain what I mean through a real story—one that I lived, not just watched from a distance.

A few years back, I got involved in a tire recycling company. The founder (I will call him T3) had been running it for over two decades. He had built it from the ground up and created a genuinely profitable operation. It was capital-intensive, highly operational, and full of moving parts—literally. Trucks, trailers, shredders, land leases, insurance requirements, and a sales cycle that required real relationship building. T3 knew his product and his customers, and he had a strong team. What he didn't have was clean accounting or a strategic capital plan.

For years, like a lot of business owners, T3 reinvested every dollar back into the business. Aside from what he took out for him and his family to live comfortably, the rest was poured into equipment, land, and expansion. On paper, the company didn't look nearly as strong as it really was. Some of that was by design. He had revenue coming in through Mexico-bound tire shipments, often in cash, and some of that wasn't fully recorded. On top of that, he ran a lot of personal expenses through the business, such as a motor home, a Corvette, pilot training, and even some off-the-books spending. To him, that was normal. He owned the whole business. But when the day came that he needed a partner, all of that came back to bite him.

The catalyst wasn't a growth opportunity or a strategic pivot. It was a divorce. His only child was finishing high school, and he and his wife, who had worked side by side with him in the company for twenty years, decided to separate. She handled all the accounting. She owned 50 percent of the company. And now she wanted to be bought out.

Like most entrepreneurs in that position, T3 wasn't sitting on enough excess cash to write her a check for half the company. That's not how he had run the business. His wealth was tied up in assets, equipment, contracts, and cash flow. He didn't want to sell the company, and he didn't want to lose control. So he hired a business broker to help him find an equity partner. Someone who could inject capital, buy out his wife, and keep the business intact.

This is where everything started to unravel.

The broker he brought in didn't know how to properly prepare the company for a growth equity presentation. The broker inflated the numbers by piling on aggressive "add-backs"—items that were supposed to reflect real profitability but weren't fully documented. That might work in a casual business sale, but it doesn't hold up under professional scrutiny. When a growth equity firm is interested in a deal, they dig deep. They examine the books. They verify every claim. And when the numbers don't line up, they walk.

Five firms issued T3 letters of interest, and three submitted formal letters of intent. One of them offered the highest valuation, and like many entrepreneurs, he went with the biggest number. On paper, it seemed like the best path forward. But he overlooked the structure, the terms, and most importantly, the fit.

When diligence began, everything fell apart. The numbers presented didn't hold up. The firm couldn't verify the add-backs, couldn't make sense of the undocumented cash flow, and couldn't get comfortable with the way expenses had been managed. After nearly a year of exhausting reviews, calls, and back-and-forth document requests, the firm came back with a revised offer: half the original valuation. The problem wasn't that the business wasn't valuable, because it was. The problem was that it wasn't presented in a way that gave investors confidence.

Here's what's important: This was not a failing company. It had a solid model, a strong customer base, and good margins. But because of the industry it operated in and the informal way it had been run, it needed a different kind of capital partner. One who could look past the messy books and see the fundamentals. One who wasn't looking for a quick exit in two or three years but was comfortable building something slower, deeper, and more sustainable.

That's why I say capital must match the business. A high-growth SaaS company might thrive under a venture model that expects a five-year exit. A tire recycling company operating across six states needs patient capital, deep operational support, and the ability to weather complexity. The structure, timeline, and expectations have to match. Otherwise, you're setting both parties up for frustration—or worse—failure.

So when entrepreneurs ask me what kind of capital they should pursue, I always ask about the business itself. What does it need? What can it handle? And who is best equipped to help it grow without breaking it apart?

The wrong capital, even when it comes with the right number, can leave you worse off than where you started.

Because the wrong capital, even when it comes with the right number, can leave you worse off than where you started.

When Capital Is Done Right

After the original deal collapsed and T3's options dried up, he came to me with a heavy heart and a business in trouble. He wasn't asking for a handout but a path forward. That's when we both learned what it looks like when capital is done right.

I had known T3 for years. We had hunted together, swapped business war stories, and shared more than a few meals over late-night fires. So when T3 called and explained the bind he was in—divorce finalized, cash wiped out, partner gone, and no serious buyers left—I knew he didn't need a buyer. He needed a builder. Someone who could help him stabilize the foundation and give him room to breathe.

I agreed to come in, not as a majority partner right away, but through a convertible note that gave him immediate working capital and some breathing room.

That initial investment was structured carefully. I took a small equity position and set terms that allowed me to convert more over time, depending on how things progressed. But more than the money, what I brought was *clarity*. The first step was to clean up the books and finance structure. The financials were a mess—more than fifty separate notes payable to various lenders, each with different terms, rates, and amortization schedules. No one could manage that many levers and keep a steady grip on the wheel. So we streamlined all of it. We refinanced everything into a clean, structured package. We introduced real accounting discipline and put reporting processes in place so the leadership team could actually see what was happening inside the business.

But the turning point wasn't just in the back office. It was in the way we deployed capital. One of the biggest operational expenses the company faced was waste. Every month, it was spending over $40,000 to dump leftover rubber shreds into landfills. It was deadweight loss—pure cost, no return. We decided to flip that equation. I helped the company invest in a single piece of equipment that cost us roughly $3.5 million. It was a significant outlay, but it changed everything. That machine took what used to be an expense and turned it into a revenue stream. Instead of paying to dispose of the shreds, we processed them into sellable material and began generating about $75,000 a month in income from it.

That single decision shifted the business model. It also unlocked scale. As we added capacity, we expanded our footprint across six states. Our trucking fleet grew from about thirty rigs to more than fifty, with over five hundred trailers running every day to collect and distribute tires and material. Volume increased, margins improved, and most importantly, the leadership team had the tools and capital to make smart decisions in real time.

What happened next is a testament to what the right partnership can do. Within three years, we had quadrupled EBITDA. That wasn't magic; it was discipline, structure, and smart reinvestment. And it wasn't just about the numbers. T3 stepped fully into his role as CEO, and his operating partner became a true second-in-command. They had gone from running the business to leading it.

Things were going well, and we were focused on growth, including a couple of strategic acquisitions that were in motion. But during one of those acquisitions, we met with the target company's largest customer. They had a reputation for being tough but fair, and we wanted to build the relationship early. Their CEO agreed to meet with us in person.

I tagged along for the meeting. What I didn't expect was who the CEO turned out to be: a former Bain Capital executive who had left to run his 120-year-old family business. We started talking, and within minutes, we both saw the potential. Our companies were a natural fit not just operationally but culturally. He understood long-term value creation, and he had already built a special-purpose investment entity to support growth in businesses like ours. What started as a vendor meeting quickly turned into a strategic conversation.

We weren't planning to sell, but sometimes the right opportunity shows up when you least expect it. After a series of discussions, we agreed to join forces. He acquired the business, and our two original partners stayed on to run the division inside the larger organization. The personal capital distribution they earned from that transaction was transformative for both of them.

They were finally able to create financial security for their families and establish generational wealth.

T3's was a business that nearly collapsed because of poor planning, then came back stronger because the right partner didn't just bring money; we brought alignment, structure, and belief.

That's what capital can do when you choose a partner who sees what the business can become and is willing to roll up their sleeves and build it with you.

Questions to Ask Before You Ask for Capital

Over the years, I've seen a pattern: Entrepreneurs often think they're chasing capital, when what they're really chasing is clarity. They want growth, they want stability, they want an edge, but they don't always know how to define it. And if you can't define what you're looking for, you're not going to know whether you've found the right partner.

Today, as the head of Ford Family Investments, I sit on the other side of the table. I meet with founders and owners all the time. Some are ready for capital, others not even close. What surprises me most is how few of them have asked themselves the hard questions before walking into the room. They've built good businesses. Sometimes great ones. But they've skipped the internal due diligence. And that's dangerous. Because if you don't know what kind of partner you need, you're going to get the wrong one.

> Entrepreneurs often think they're chasing capital, when what they're really chasing is clarity.

So here's what I tell every entrepreneur before they even think about raising capital: Go through this mental checklist, line by line, and be brutally honest with yourself. These aren't academic questions. They're make-or-break questions. And if you don't like your answers, don't go looking for capital just yet. Fix what needs fixing first.

ARE YOUR FINANCIALS CLEAN AND GAAP-COMPLIANT?

This doesn't mean making sure your books are tidy. It's about whether an outside party can step into your business and understand it without a two-year forensic audit. If you're still running on QuickBooks without accrual accounting or clean monthly closes, that's going to be a problem. Capital partners don't invest in stories; they invest in data they can trust.

ARE YOU RUNNING PERSONAL EXPENSES THROUGH THE BUSINESS?

I get it. When you're the founder, it all feels like one pot. But the moment you want a partner, especially an equity partner, you've got to separate church and state. The truck, the vacation home, the boat, the side-by-side—if it's not driving real business value, it shouldn't be buried in your P&L. It might save you a little on taxes today, but it's going to cost you a lot in enterprise value tomorrow.

DO YOU HAVE DOCUMENTED ADD-BACKS?

If you're planning to adjust EBITDA to reflect one-time costs or personal expenses, you'd better be ready to prove every one of them. It's not enough to say, "That number's not real." You have to explain why, and you have to back it up with clean documentation. Your buyer or investor isn't going to take your word for it; they're going to ask for a trail.

WHAT'S YOUR REAL EBITDA ... AND CAN YOU PROVE IT?

Forget the headline number. What's the real, recurring, normalized EBITDA that a capital partner can rely on going forward? Have you stripped out the noise, adjusted for seasonality, and built a forward-looking view that holds water under scrutiny? If you can't answer that with confidence, you're not ready to have the conversation.

WHAT DO YOU WANT FROM THE RELATIONSHIP BESIDES MONEY?

Money is the easy part. What else do you need? Operational support? Strategic M&A experience? HR, legal, IT, finance? Or do you want a silent partner who stays out of your way? Be honest about what you want. Otherwise, you'll end up frustrated, and so will your partner.

WHAT HAPPENS IF YOUR PARTNER ASKS FOR CONTROL? ARE YOU OK WITH THAT?

This is where ego meets reality. Control doesn't always mean day-to-day involvement, but if someone's writing a big check, they're going to expect influence. If you're not ready to share decision-making or sit across from someone who asks tough questions, you're not ready for an equity partner.

WHAT DOES AN EXIT LOOK LIKE, AND WHEN WOULD IT OCCUR?

This might be the most overlooked question of all. Are you building to hold? Building to sell? Do you want a second bite at the apple? Or are you looking for a clean walkaway? Your partner's timeline matters. If you want ten years and they want five, that's going to cause friction. Make sure your long-term goals align.

ARE YOU READY FOR SIX TO TWELVE MONTHS OF DILIGENCE?

Diligence is a process, not a formality. A grueling one. If you're not ready to live in spreadsheets, pull five years of records, and answer the same question from six different angles, it's going to be a painful experience. Prepare now, or you'll regret it later.

CAN YOU TAKE A HARD LOOK AT YOUR NUMBERS AND LIVE WITH THEM?

Your business might be growing. It might be profitable. But it's also imperfect. Can you be honest about the weak spots? Can you handle the feedback without getting defensive? Because any good capital partner is going to find the cracks, and if you're not ready to own them, you're not ready to grow.

WOULD YOU WORK FOR YOUR PARTNER IF THE TABLES WERE TURNED?

This is the ultimate test. If the deal flipped—if you were the minority owner and they were in charge—would you still want to show up every day? Would you trust them with your team, your customers, your culture? If the answer is no, walk away. No amount of money is worth a bad fit.

> Capital doesn't fix a business. It just amplifies whatever's already there.

The truth is that capital doesn't fix a business. It just amplifies whatever's already there.

If your business is strong and your leadership is grounded, capital can take you to the next level. But if you're running sloppily, chasing shortcuts, or dodging hard conversations, it'll expose every flaw you've tried to hide.

So, before you seek out a partner, ask yourself the questions they're going to ask. Do your own diligence. Know what you want. Know what you're offering. And above all, choose with intention.

Capital, when done right, doesn't just grow your business. It grows your impact. But only if you're ready for it.

TIMELESS TAKEAWAYS

1. Every dollar comes with a perspective, a personality, and a point of view. Too many entrepreneurs treat capital like a commodity—something to be priced and accepted based on terms alone. But when you take on a capital partner, you're entering into a long-term relationship. You're giving them a seat at your table and a say in how your business evolves. If the alignment isn't there, the deal won't just underperform; it will unravel. The best capital partners don't just write checks; they challenge your thinking, support your team, and stand by you when the road gets bumpy. The wrong ones bring control issues, mismatched expectations, and short-term thinking that can damage what you've spent years building. Choose accordingly.

2. Entrepreneurs often chase capital in moments of pressure: a big opportunity, a liquidity event, or a personal crisis. But if you haven't clarified what kind of capital you need—and why—you're likely to make the wrong choice. Do you need speed or stability? A silent partner or an active operator? Are you looking to sell in three years or build something that lasts thirty? Just like you wouldn't walk into a restaurant and simply ask for "food," you shouldn't walk into a pitch meeting just asking for "capital." Be specific. The clearer you are about what you need, the more likely you are to attract a partner who fits. Capital follows clarity, but it also demands character. If you're not ready to be transparent, structured, and accountable, then you're not ready for the right kind of capital.

3. There is no universal capital playbook. What fuels a SaaS company may smother a tire recycling business. The nature of your industry—its pace, complexity, capital intensity, and operating model—should dictate the kind of investment you pursue. Don't chase the structure that worked for someone else unless your business shares their DNA. A venture-backed structure may make sense for a high-growth tech startup, but it will likely strain a multilocation services business with heavy equipment and long sales cycles. Align capital to context. The right partner will see the business for what it is (and what it could become) and structure the investment accordingly. When capital fits the business, it unlocks growth. When it doesn't, it builds tension and forces compromise.

CHAPTER FIVE

MONETIZING YOUR BUSINESS

*You should run your business as if you were going
to own it forever—but be ready to sell it tomorrow.*

—WARREN BUFFETT

In the spring of 2009, I was sitting across from a distressed man
in Madrid, Spain. The economy was still bleeding from the global
financial crisis, and automotive dealerships across America were
carrying debt they could no longer afford. He was the owner of a
once-thriving group of two stores, and he needed an exit. Fast.

I was there on behalf of Sonic Automotive, representing the
company with one of our auto manufacturing partners who was
showing us new products that were coming out over the next
twenty-four months. This particular portfolio looked attractive from
the outside—multiple rooftops, premium brands, and a strong geo-
graphic footprint. But the minute we got into the numbers, it became
clear: The deal was never going to happen.

At first glance, the failure to close might seem like a dead end. But in hindsight, it marked the beginning of something far more important. That failed transaction forced me to look at the business through a different lens. It was the first time I began to think like an investor, not just a deal guy.

Back then, I was still steeped in the operations side of the business. My world was built on margins, inventory turns, fixed ops performance, and hitting monthly forecasts. But this deal forced a shift. I couldn't just evaluate the business based on operational performance. I had to think in terms of risk. Structure. Return on capital. I had to understand what wasn't being said, essentially what *wasn't* on the balance sheet but should've been.

The business was located in Texas, and it had potential. On paper, it had the right brands, the right markets, and the right customer base. But underneath the surface, it was a house of cards. The financials were muddy, the documentation was incomplete, and the liabilities far outweighed any potential upside. There was no clean path to a turnaround, and even if we had moved forward, the cost of unwinding the debt alone would have crippled our return.

What struck me most at the time was that the seller genuinely didn't understand why his business wasn't sellable. He'd built a respectable company by normal standards. He knew his customer base. He was in desirable locations. However, when it came to capital structure, investor expectations, and what a buyer was really looking for, he was flying blind. And I don't say that as a criticism. It's actually more common than most founders realize.

That moment stuck with me. I found myself revisiting the experience over and over. What went wrong? What was missing? And more importantly, what would it have taken to make that deal work?

It became clear that the business itself wasn't the real problem. The problem was the disconnect between what the seller thought his business was worth and what the market was actually willing to pay. And that gap came down to preparation. Not in the traditional sense of better marketing or a sharper presentation, but financial literacy, transparency, and strategic positioning.

If the seller had understood what really drives valuation, he might have made different decisions in the years leading up to that moment and avoided some of the structural mistakes that made his company uninvestable. That was a turning point for me. It was the moment I realized that successful exits aren't born from last-minute maneuvers but from long-term preparation.

> Successful exits aren't born from last-minute maneuvers but from long-term preparation.

As I continued to grow in my career and eventually built RFJ Auto Partners, I kept that Madrid story in the back of my mind. Every time I evaluated a new opportunity, I asked myself: *What would I see if I were on the other side of the table? Where are the risks? Where are the gaps? Is this business truly built for an investor or just for the founder?*

Years later, when I started working with smaller business owners through Ford Family Investments, I saw the same pattern repeat itself. Founders with good businesses, strong customer loyalty, and years of hard work under their belt but no framework for understanding how their company would be evaluated by the outside world. Many of them had never even heard the term *EBITDA*, much less understood how to calculate it accurately. Others ran perfectly legal—but highly opaque—books, mixing personal and business expenses, relying on add-backs that couldn't be substantiated, or failing to maintain a clean, GAAP-compliant financial trail.

The danger in all of this isn't just that a deal falls apart. The real cost is *time*. When a buyer gets serious, due diligence starts immediately. And if a founder isn't ready, meaning if the data can't be trusted,

> The danger in all of this isn't just that a deal falls apart. The real cost is *time*.

if the team isn't strong, if the story doesn't hold up under pressure, then the window of opportunity closes quickly. Even worse, word gets around.

In the world of growth capital, reputation travels fast. One failed process can put you on a "Do not touch" list that takes years to escape.

That deal in Madrid may have been a miss, but it gave me something more valuable than any commission check. It gave me the perspective I needed to become a better builder, and eventually, a better partner to the entrepreneurs I work with today.

From Operator to Opportunist

The moment I started thinking like an investor, I couldn't unsee the white space. I'd spent the better part of three decades operating inside dealership groups, building stores, managing people, and squeezing out efficiency. But once the lens shifted, I started to see something different. The real opportunity wasn't in running better stores, but in *owning* them. Not just one or two, but dozens.

At the time, dealership ownership in the US was still highly fragmented. Thousands of stores were still operated by independent family businesses, many of them led by aging founders with no succession plan and an eye on retirement. Valuations were low, still bruised from the Great Recession, and sellers were getting anxious. These weren't necessarily broken businesses. Most of them were steady, profitable, and deeply entrenched in their local markets. What they lacked was a buyer who could see the bigger picture.

That's when the roll-up strategy started to take shape in my mind. The idea wasn't revolutionary; after all, industries consolidate all the time. But it hadn't yet taken hold in automotive retail the way it had in other sectors. The few large public groups had already scooped up the obvious targets, and the rest of the market remained wide open. There was an opportunity in the middle: the stores that were too big for the mom-and-pop buyers but too small to attract the attention of Wall Street.

Still, it was one thing to see the opportunity and another to act on it. I had a good job. Sonic Automotive gave me real responsibility, access to sophisticated systems, and a front-row seat to how a national operation worked. I was making good money and learning from smart people who treated me well and who truly cared about their people. But deep down, I knew I wasn't building something of my own. I was helping someone else execute their vision. For me, that wasn't going to be enough.

The turning point came over lunch.

I had a long-standing relationship with a real estate investor who also served on a charitable board with me. We were catching up when I mentioned this idea I'd been kicking around—a hypothesis about fragmented ownership, depressed valuations, and the potential for consolidation. He asked a few questions, nodded slowly, then said something I'll never forget: "If you really believe this, why aren't you raising capital and doing it yourself?"

He wasn't joking, but I laughed anyway. At the time, I didn't know the first thing about raising money. I wasn't a Wall Street guy. I didn't have a finance pedigree. I hadn't gone to Harvard or Stanford. I was an operator, nothing more, nothing less. But he kept pushing.

"You don't *need* to know everything," he said. "You just need to know what you're building. Start there."

So I did. That night, I went home and opened PowerPoint. I didn't even know what to call the file—"pitch_deck_v1" seemed good enough. It wasn't much to look at: a handful of slides about dealership economics, a few back-of-the-napkin projections, and a long list of unanswered questions. But it was a start. And it gave me something to talk about when I started making calls.

The early conversations were rough. I didn't know the language of capital. Terms such as *preferred equity, waterfall structure,* and *hurdle rate* were foreign to me. I'd walk into meetings thinking I was pitching an investment idea, only to realize I was being evaluated just as much as the idea itself. Who was I? What was my track record? What did I know about managing capital, or risk for that matter?

Every meeting was a master class. I asked questions and definitely listened more than I talked. Slowly, I started to understand what mattered to investors and how to position the opportunity in a way that made sense to them. It wasn't about projecting unending growth or offering guarantees but showing that I understood the business cold and had the operational chops, the market insight, and the willingness to put my own skin in the game.

Still, it wasn't easy to walk away from security. Leaving Sonic meant stepping into the unknown without the assurance that anyone would write a check, much less back a roll-up strategy with a national footprint. But if I'd learned anything from that failed deal in Madrid, it was this: Waiting for certainty is the

> Waiting for certainty is the fastest way to miss an opportunity. You have to move when the conditions are right, not when everything is perfect.

fastest way to miss an opportunity. You have to move when the conditions are right, not when everything is perfect.

So I resigned. There was no grand send-off or fanfare. Just a quiet acknowledgment that I was leaving something good in pursuit of something better.

From that point forward, my life shifted into a different gear. I was building a business instead of operating one. I was laying the foundation for what would become RFJ Auto Partners. It didn't happen overnight. It took years of grinding, raising capital, and proving the model one acquisition at a time.

Valuation Is Neither Universal nor Objective

One of the biggest mistakes entrepreneurs make is assuming there's a standard formula for what their business is worth. That it's just math. A clean EBITDA figure, a simple multiple, a fair number pops out, and that's the price. But valuation doesn't work like that, not in the real world. It's not just a function of earnings or even growth but a subjective exercise shaped by who's buying, why they're buying, and what kind of business you're actually running.

When I first started looking at businesses through an investor's lens, this became painfully clear. In the automotive world, for example, we don't just talk about multiples of EBITDA. We talk about "blue sky." That's our shorthand for goodwill, the premium value over the tangible assets. And it's often the number owners focus on most. They'll say, "What's my blue sky?" not, "What's my balance sheet worth?" That number is usually based on a multiple of earnings, yes, but even that multiple is up for debate. It can swing widely depending on the brand, location, and even macroeconomic conditions.

I've seen valuations calculated using a straight average of the last three years' earnings. I've also seen weighted models, where the most recent year carries more influence than years prior. And in some cases, buyers want a five-year picture, especially if they're trying to smooth out a volatile earnings history. But what everyone is really trying to understand is the *consistency* of earnings. Are they stable? Growing? Declining?

The worst scenario you can find yourself in is what we used to call a "falling knife," a business with earnings that are headed south without a clear reason (I want to give credit to one of my partners and also now one of my closest friends—Eion Hu with The Jordan Company, now TJC—who introduced this term to me). If your trend line is negative, you'd better be able to explain it. I've lived through enough cycles—'08, '09, the first year of COVID-19—to know that external shocks happen. Investors don't expect you to be invincible. But they do expect you to know your numbers and your story.

Consistency matters. So does the quality of your earnings. In asset-heavy businesses, there's another key factor: *free cash flow*. Most operators get stuck obsessing over their P&L, but it's the cash flow statement that tells the truth about a business. How much cash is left over after taxes, debt service, and capital expenditures (CapEx)? That's the number that equity investors really care about because it tells them what they'll have to reinvest in the business or take out of it.

Depreciation plays a huge role in that equation. If you're in a capital-intensive industry, like we were in recycling, you might be spending millions on equipment, and that investment shows up as depreciation on your books. For tax purposes, that can be a good thing. There were years when we made full use of bonus depreciation, which allowed us to deduct the entire cost of an asset in the year we bought it. I remember when we bought a $3.5 million machine in the recycling business. Thanks to the legislation at the time, we got to take the full depreciation that year, which dramatically lowered our taxable income and boosted our free cash flow.

That impacts your bottom line *and* directly influences your valuation. If you're generating strong free cash after CapEx and taxes, your business becomes more attractive to buyers, especially those focused on cash-on-cash returns.

And that's another point that often gets missed: *Who* is valuing your business matters as much as *how* they're doing it. A PE firm is going to look at things differently from how a family office will. They have different timelines, different return expectations, and different tolerances for reinvestment. A PE group might ask you to roll earnings back into the business to keep scaling. A family office may want steady distributions.

Real estate investors apply another lens altogether. In that world, valuations are driven more by cap rates and lease structures than by earnings. It's about predictable rental income and risk-adjusted returns. If your business owns its own real estate, that becomes a separate valuation conversation. You may be better off selling the business and leasing the property back, rather than bundling everything into one deal.

The key is knowing whom you're talking to and what matters to them. There's no one-size-fits-all approach. What looks like a high multiple in one industry may be standard in another. What's considered a clean deal to one investor might feel risky to another. That's why you can't rely on back-of-the-envelope math or internet benchmarks.

> The key is knowing whom you're talking to and what matters to them. There's no one-size-fits-all approach.

I tell entrepreneurs this all the time: Talk to people in your industry who have sold. Ask what their multiple was. More importantly, ask *why* they got that multiple. Was it because of consistent growth? Limited competition? Favorable real estate terms? A deep bench of management talent?

You can't control every factor, but you can control how well you understand your business. If you want to monetize it properly, whether next year or ten years from now, then you have to know how it will be valued. That means digging into your cash flow, keeping your financials tight, and understanding how outside investors will view your earnings, assets, and growth potential.

Because valuation isn't just a number; it's a narrative. And the better you know your story, the more likely you are to write your own positive ending.

What Investors Really See

One of the biggest mental shifts I had to make when stepping into the investment world was realizing that value doesn't always equal profit. I had spent my entire career thinking in terms of monthly statements—what came in, what went out, what was left over. But the lens I had trained myself to use as an operator wasn't the same lens investors used. They weren't just looking at income statements. They were looking at everything: balance sheets, depreciation schedules, CapEx forecasts, real estate footprints, and even something as small as the age of our HVAC units.

That shift in perspective was both humbling and eye-opening. It's one thing to build a successful business. It's another thing to make it attractive to someone who might want to buy it. Investors don't just look at how much money your business is making today. They look at how much money it might make, or cost, tomorrow.

Take depreciation, for example. Most small business owners treat it as a line item that their accountants explain at tax time. But serious investors study it closely. They want to know how much of your earnings are real and how much are being masked or inflated by the way you've handled asset purchases. A new facility or piece of machinery might provide a tax advantage in the short term, but it also changes your long-term cost structure.

CapEx needs are another area that separates operational thinking from investor thinking. A business might be profitable today, but if its assets are aging and replacement costs are looming, that profit may be short-lived. Investors want to know how much you're going to have to reinvest just to maintain your current output. They want to understand your maintenance backlog, your equipment life cycle, and how much cash you'll need to deploy over the next five years.

This came into sharp focus for me when I started walking investors through RFJ's assets. I had to break it down piece by piece. In the dealership world, valuation comes from four core areas: blue sky, real estate, inventory, and fixed assets.

BLUE SKY (MORE COMMONLY KNOWN AS GOODWILL)

Blue sky is the premium someone is willing to pay for the brand, the customer base, and the leadership team you've built. It is basically paying for expected future earnings. It's not on the balance sheet, but it's often the largest piece of the deal. If your team is high-performing and your customer base is loyal, that blue sky can drive real value. But it's fragile. One change in leadership or a dip in customer satisfaction can take it down quickly.

REAL ESTATE

Real estate is another major component. But not all real estate is created equal. A Ford dealership in suburban Texas, where land is cheaper and demand is high, is worth more than the exact same operation in downtown San Francisco. Why? Because the overhead in San Francisco is through the roof, the regulations are tighter, and the path to profitability is longer.

Investors evaluate real estate using cap rates, which help them determine the expected return based on the income the property can generate. A property that produces steady rental income in a low-risk market commands a different cap rate than one in a volatile or declining area. It's all about risk-adjusted returns. So, even if you've got prime square footage, if it's in a market that's losing population or facing regulatory headwinds, your value takes a hit.

INVENTORY

Inventory is the next big lever. In our business, inventory means vehicles. But holding too much inventory, especially when financing is tight, can work against you. Investors want to know how fast your inventory turns and what kind of carrying costs are involved. A bloated inventory might look like strength to a novice, but to an investor, it might signal inefficiency or weak demand.

FIXED ASSETS

Finally, there are fixed assets—furniture, fixtures, and equipment. These are the tangible parts of the business that age and require upkeep. The question investors ask is simple: How much of what I'm buying is going to break down, wear out, or need to be replaced?

All this came into play when I began positioning RFJ for outside capital. I had to help investors *see* the value the way we experienced it on the ground, but through their lens. That meant translating operational success into financial clarity. I couldn't just say, "This is a great store." I had to show *why*, backed by data, projections, and a deep understanding of the underlying assets.

Those underlying assets were only part of the story. Macro trends were shifting fast. The rise of electric vehicles, new environmental policies, and changing consumer preferences were external factors that could swing valuations in ways we couldn't control. A brand that had been highly desirable five years ago might suddenly fall out of favor. Conversely, a lesser-known brand in a growth market might jump in value just because of its future positioning.

Investors track those trends closely. They look at regulation, infrastructure, supply chains, and even political sentiment. That's why staying informed and adaptable needs to be a part of every valuation strategy.

If there's one thing I've learned, it's this: The value of your business isn't just in what it does. It's in what someone else sees it can do. That means understanding how to build a business and how to present it clearly, credibly, and with a level of transparency that builds trust. Because until someone else sees the value, it's not value you can monetize.

> The value of your business isn't just in what it does. It's in what someone else sees it can do.

Build to Exit, Even If You Never Exit

One of the biggest mistakes I see business owners make is assuming that an exit is either too far away to worry about or something that simply doesn't apply to them. They tell themselves, *I'm not building to sell*, or *This is a legacy business*, or *I'll figure that out when the time comes.* But the time rarely announces itself with a neat little memo. More often, it shows up disguised as something else—a health scare, a family change, a shift in the market. And when that day arrives, if you haven't built your business with optionality in mind, you'll find yourself scrambling.

Even if you never intend to sell, you should build as if you will. That mindset forces you to think differently about the decisions you're making today. It sharpens your discipline. It brings clarity to the way you spend money, structure teams, and track performance. It pushes you to create documentation around what's working and why, because when the day comes that someone else needs to understand your business quickly, that paper trail becomes essential.

In the last chapter, I described how I've seen firsthand how critical that kind of foresight can be with my friend's tire recycling business. He had built a solid operation, turning scrap tires into usable material, and the business had great potential. But it was costing him $40,000 a month in landfill fees just to dispose of the byproduct his equipment couldn't process. That recurring expense was dragging down his margins and limiting his ability to grow.

Within a year, that $3.5 million investment into a new piece of equipment turned into a complete shift in his business model. Instead of spending $40,000 a month, the company began generating $75,000 a month in new revenue. The team expanded into six states. The trucking fleet grew. EBITDA quadrupled. And when we began having serious conversations with a potential acquirer, we were able to point to every decision, every investment, and every outcome—not just through memory or anecdote but through detailed, well-organized documentation.

That's what buyers want. Not just a good story, but evidence. They want to see that your business is built on more than instinct or relationships. They want to know that you've made intentional decisions and that those decisions have paid off or, if they haven't, that you've adjusted and learned. They want confidence that they're stepping into a system, not a personality.

And the truth is, circumstances change. You might think your kids will take over the business someday, but that decision isn't entirely up to you. I've known plenty of owners who assumed the next generation would step in, only to discover their children had no interest. Some realized it too late, and the business deteriorated without a plan. Others were able to adapt because they'd already built with optionality in mind.

Economic conditions can shift just as quickly. Markets turn. Lending tightens. Supply chains collapse. I've lived through enough downturns to know that timing isn't always in your control. If you want to have the choice to sell or partner or scale, you have to prepare in advance.

That doesn't mean running your business like a robot. It means treating your business like an investment and always looking at your decisions through two lenses: What's right for the business today? And how will this look to someone evaluating the business tomorrow?

Ask yourself: *If I left the business tomorrow, could someone else step in and understand why I made the decisions I did? Could they see the long game I was playing? Could they pick up where I left off and move the business forward?*

> It means treating your business like an investment and always looking at your decisions through two lenses: What's right for the business today? And how will this look to someone evaluating the business tomorrow?

If the answer is no, you've got work to do. And the sooner you start, the more valuable your business becomes, whether or not you ever choose to sell.

Infrastructure = Value

One of the first things I listen for when talking to a founder is what would happen if they stepped away from the business for a week or more. Not a vacation with a laptop in their bag. A real break. No calls. No texts. Just a clean handoff and a quiet phone. If their answer is anything other than complete confidence, we're probably not looking at a scalable business. We're looking at a job they've built for themselves.

That might sound harsh, but it's reality. And this bears repeating: At Ford Family Investments, we often say that *we invest in the jockey, not the horse*. But the full truth is this: The best jockeys don't just ride well. *They train others to ride.* They build systems and teams that can run without them and make themselves replaceable.

Too many entrepreneurs wear their irreplaceability like a badge of honor. They'll tell you they're the only ones who can close the big deals, calm down the toughest customer, or sign off on critical decisions. Maybe they're right. But that doesn't make their business more valuable. It makes it fragile.

When we evaluated the tire recycling business we ultimately helped transform and sell, that founder was on the phone every hunting trip. No matter where he went, he was tied to the operation. He couldn't unplug without the fear that something would go sideways. There wasn't a number two, and there weren't any well-documented processes in place for the people below him to confidently follow. It was a one-man machine.

For a while, it worked. He made money. He kept things moving. But it wasn't sustainable. He was burning out, and the business wasn't set up to thrive without him. That became painfully clear when he tried to exit. The initial buyer came in, saw how dependent the company was on a single person, and backed away. The risk was too high. The systems weren't built. There was no succession path. There was no real infrastructure.

I see this more often than I'd like to admit. Founders are so deep in the day-to-day that they never build the systems that allow them to step away. They haven't written down the processes. They haven't delegated real authority. They haven't trained leaders to make decisions without checking in. Sometimes it's ego. Sometimes it's fear. Sometimes it's just habit. But the result is the same: a business that looks busy but isn't truly built with an eye toward scale.

Here's the shift that has to happen: You have to start seeing your role not as the driver of everything, but as the architect of something bigger than yourself. If you can't take a five-day vacation without your business falling apart, then you don't own a business. You own a job with overhead and risk.

Real infrastructure is what creates real value. That's what capital partners are buying. They're betting on the machine, not just the founder's stamina. They want to know that if you won the lottery or had a significant health issue—or, more realistically, if you decide to do something else in five years—the business wouldn't skip a beat. It would keep generating cash flow, keep growing, and keep operating with the same values and consistency you built it on.

> If you can't take a five-day vacation without your business falling apart, then you don't own a business. You own a job with overhead and risk.

That's why leadership depth matters. That's why documentation matters. That's why cross-training matters. The more your business can function without you, the more valuable it becomes to everyone—investors, customers, and future employees alike.

In our work, we often assess whether an operator has invested in creating a real leadership bench. Have they taken the time to develop their managers? Can their CFO explain the financial model without the founder in the room? Can the operations team walk through their KPIs and performance plans without needing to check back? These questions are deal-breakers.

One of the turning points for the recycling business came when we helped them build out real infrastructure. We invested in talent and documented every core function. We created clear reporting lines and KPIs. We empowered managers to make decisions, and we created accountability mechanisms that didn't require the founder to be the bottleneck. Over time, the founder went from being on every call to focusing on strategy, growth, and relationships, the places where he created the most value. That shift reduced his stress *and* raised the business's valuation.

Here's the truth no one wants to hear: Your exit isn't just a financial transaction. It's a referendum on how well you built the business. If it can't survive without you, it's not ready for a buyer or even an equity partner. Even if you never plan to sell, what happens if life throws you a curveball? What happens if you need to step back sooner than expected?

Infrastructure is the insurance policy. It's the bridge between a busy operation and a truly valuable enterprise. Build it now before you need it. Your future self will thank you.

TIMELESS TAKEAWAYS

1. Most entrepreneurs think of value in terms of income, profit margins, or customer loyalty, but capital partners view value through the lens of transferability. If the business relies too heavily on you (the founder) for decision-making, relationships, or execution, then it's not a business. It's a job with a fancy title. The more your company depends on your daily presence, the less scalable and salable it becomes. True enterprise value is built when you create systems, develop leaders, and document processes in a way that allows the business to function without you. That's the foundation of sustainable growth.

2. Valuation is a dynamic, situational exercise shaped by your industry, your buyer, and the unique narrative behind your business. EBITDA matters, but so does the quality of your earnings, the structure of your balance sheet, the health of your team, and the credibility of your financials. Two companies with similar numbers can receive wildly different valuations based on risk, growth potential, infrastructure, and the confidence a buyer has in what's under the hood. Your job as a founder is to tell that story with clarity and conviction, then back it up with data that builds trust. The stronger the narrative and the cleaner the facts, the more leverage you'll have when the real negotiations begin.

3. Exits rarely happen on your schedule. Illness, market shifts, personal changes, or unsolicited offers can all force your hand. If your business isn't ready when opportunity (or necessity) shows up, you'll miss your window, or worse, be forced into a deal you regret. That's why you need to build with optionality from day one. Treat your business like an investment, not just a paycheck. Clean up your financials. Document your decisions. Create a leadership bench. Structure your business so it's always ready to withstand scrutiny. Even if you never sell, you'll be better protected, more resilient, and more in control of your own destiny.

THE FOUR-YEAR "OVERNIGHT" SUCCESS

The man on top of the mountain didn't fall there.

—VINCE LOMBARDI

When I left Sonic in 2010, it wasn't because I had a detailed plan for what came next. It was simply time. I had spent nearly three decades in auto retail, navigating everything from day-to-day store operations to broader strategy at the executive level. I had learned a great deal, contributed at a high level, and earned the respect of peers across the industry. But I felt an urge to build something of my own—something I could guide from the ground up, shaped not by a boardroom or shareholder demands, but by clear operating principles and a long-term vision.

At first, the decision to step away felt like I was simply closing a chapter. It wasn't until I started receiving calls from industry contacts that I realized another chapter might already be starting. Several dealers, still recovering from the 2008–2009 financial crisis, were exploring options. Some were ready to exit. Others were hanging on, but without much enthusiasm for rebuilding. In most cases, they were looking for someone who could purchase the business and lead it with care. Someone who understood operations, culture, and the balance sheet.

These conversations caught my attention. I wasn't in a position to acquire anything yet, but the pattern was unmistakable. There were real opportunities surfacing in the wake of the downturn. Public companies were sitting still, reluctant to expand while their stock prices were under pressure. Outside equity capital hadn't yet turned its attention to the sector in a meaningful way. And yet, here was a window, a brief moment when the right operator, with the right capital partner, could build a substantial platform.

That window started to take on greater urgency during the trip to Spain, as mentioned in an earlier chapter. Although that acquisition ultimately didn't work out, it got me thinking: *What if?* I didn't have the structure, capital, or team in place to pursue it, but I realized that if I didn't move quickly, I might miss the window to launch something new altogether. By the end of that trip, I was resolved about what had been building inside me for months. I had to stop treating the urge to start my own business like a thought exercise. It was time to commit.

My first instinct was to bring the idea back to Sonic and see if there was interest in collaborating on a new venture. I knew the team well, and I believed there was mutual respect. But their hands were tied. The market wasn't rewarding growth at the time, and they had to prioritize short-term stability. That left me looking elsewhere.

I had no experience raising capital, at least not in the formal sense. But I did have relationships. I reached out to a few trusted contacts, including a longtime friend in the real estate sector. Through that connection, I was introduced to a Fort Worth–based family office that had invested in the automotive industry before, understood the space, and was open to a conversation.

I laid out a vision that wasn't based on financial projections or elaborate models. What I offered was a disciplined, operations-first strategy built around acquiring strong businesses and running them better. I had no stores at that point. No cash flow. No assets on paper. What I had was a reputation earned over decades of delivering results, building strong teams, and managing with integrity. That's what they were evaluating: my track record.

The conversations progressed quickly. What became clear was that this family office wasn't looking for a flashy operator or a short-term return. It wanted a long-term partner who would run the business the right way, stay focused on fundamentals, and communicate with honesty. That was a fit I could work with, even though the office was only looking to invest $15 million–$25 million over several years (see the earlier chapter about the "right" fit).

That moment marked the true beginning of what would become RFJ. It didn't feel dramatic. There was no big announcement, no media story, and no public launch. What existed then was a commitment from me, a vision, and a group of people who believed it was possible. Every other piece—the platform, the process, the results— would have to be built from scratch.

I've had people tell me over the years that they always expected I'd eventually go out on my own. Some even said it seemed inevitable. But it didn't feel that way at the time. Every step forward required conviction, patience, and a willingness to embrace risk. I wasn't stepping into an existing structure or taking over a mature business. I was standing at the edge of something that didn't exist yet, with no guarantee it would work. And I was OK with that. Because what mattered to me was that it would be mine to build, start to finish.

Vision with Nothing Behind It

When I set out to raise the capital for RFJ, I had no assets to speak of. No legacy business I could point to as collateral. What I did have was a vision for what could be built, a well-earned reputation for running operations with discipline, and a set of deeply held convictions about what kind of company I wanted to create. That was it.

I knew what I was asking for was bold. I needed an approximately $150 million commitment to get started, and I was doing it without any hard leverage to offer in return. But I also knew that the right partners wouldn't be investing in the existing balance sheet or P&L that would become RFJ. They would be investing in who was behind it: the jockey, not the horse. And while that line gets repeated often, I learned just how real it is when you're standing in front of a room trying to raise money with nothing to show but your résumé and a whiteboard.

The people who chose to back me weren't doing so because I had promised outsized returns or flashy projections. They did it because they knew who I was, how I operated, and what I stood for. That's what gave them confidence. Not the pitch itself, but the history behind it.

One of the earliest affirmations I received came from Jeff Dyke, who at the time was a colleague and my boss at Sonic and someone I respected immensely. Jeff had seen me in action. He knew the way I thought about customers, the way I ran stores, and the way I built teams. His encouragement for me was a moment of quiet confidence. When someone you respect looks at your idea and says, "You're the one to do this," it matters.

Mike Maroone was another person whose belief meant a lot. Mike had seen the good and the bad in this industry. He had weathered downturns, managed growth, and earned his scars the hard way. So when he told me he believed in what I was building, it wasn't casual. It came from experience, from someone who understood how rare it was to find a leader who could combine execution with vision.

But belief from mentors, no matter how meaningful, still had to be matched by belief in myself. Because what I was really doing wasn't just raising capital but making a bet on my own future. *Without* a safety net.

Leaving a stable corporate path is never easy. I could have stayed where I was, remained in a senior role, and continued drawing a comfortable salary with predictable bonuses. There's nothing wrong with that choice. For many people, it's the smart move. But I had reached a point where staying put would have meant turning away from something I felt called to do.

RFJ was never meant to be a single-store operation. It wasn't about controlling one location or replicating a model that already existed. From the beginning, the goal was to build a platform, something that could scale with integrity, that could grow without compromising on quality, and that could deliver strong financial returns while honoring the people who made those returns possible.

People started paying attention when we hit twenty-four dealerships in our first twenty-four months. That's when the headlines began. That's when the phone started ringing with reporters and industry people wanting to know how we'd pulled it off. But what they didn't see was the four years before we bought our first store. From the outside, it looked like we came out of nowhere. But the truth is, the real work started long before there was anything to show for it.

RFJ didn't begin with a ribbon-cutting or a press release. It began in early 2010, with me sitting at a desk with a blank piece of paper and a long list of things that needed to be built before we could even begin. At that point, I had the vision, I had a few early commitments, and I had a rough map of where I wanted to go. But the business itself was still just a framework. The next four years would be about turning that framework into something that could actually support growth.

That meant legal infrastructure had to be locked in from day one. We weren't going to be flipping one store or playing around the edges of the industry. This was a platform strategy, and that meant we had to think at scale, even when the operation was still theoretical. We built out holding companies, created a repeatable acquisition template, and structured the parent entity in a way that would be attractive to future capital partners and lenders. Those were the decisions that no one saw, but they set the tone for everything that followed.

On the capital side, we worked through multiple models to understand how equity would be deployed, how it would be tracked, and how it would come back. The capital structure had to support repeat transactions, with clarity around returns and reinvestment opportunities. We were raising money for a sequence of deals that would stack on top of each other, with each layer building toward something bigger. That takes time. And patience. And it takes people willing to fund a vision that hasn't yet produced a dollar of revenue.

One of the tools that emerged from that period was something we called the Commitment Tracker. It was a simple idea, but a powerful one. Every dollar of equity we raised was tracked in real time—when it was committed, when it was deployed, and when it started returning. I wanted to be able to sit across from a partner and show them, line by line, where their money was going and what it was doing. That level of transparency built trust, and that trust became one of the biggest assets we had in those early years.

We also spent that time building out the deal flow pipeline. Acquisitions don't happen by accident. You have to know who's thinking about selling, who's quietly testing the market, and who might be open to a conversation under the right circumstances. That's a long game. It's phone calls. It's meetings that go nowhere. It's waiting six months to hear back. But it's also where momentum is built. By the time we were ready to transact, we had a pipeline in place and were positioned to move quickly.

Then, in July of 2014, everything hit at once. We closed our first set of acquisitions—seven dealerships in thirty days. That alone would've been a fast start for any new company. But we didn't stop there. The systems we had built behind the scenes gave us the ability to move faster than most people thought was possible. Over the next twenty-four months, we went from zero to twenty-four rooftops. The media loved that. However, behind the catchy headline was four years of planning, mapping, and refining every single process.

Those first two years postlaunch were when the theoretical became real. That's when we began learning, in real time, how our assumptions would hold up. One of the biggest early lessons came in understanding the role of real estate. Dealership profitability is one thing, but the value of the underlying real estate—location, ownership structure, cost basis—can shape the economics of a deal in ways many operators overlook. I had to get fluent in those mechanics quickly.

We also learned how complex consolidation could be. When you're acquiring family-owned businesses, you're not just buying operations; you're stepping into cultures, personalities, and long-standing systems that don't always translate. The back-office work was harder than we expected. Merging accounting systems, aligning HR processes, and creating standardized reporting didn't happen overnight. We got better each time, but the learning curve was steep.

Still, even with all those challenges, we were doing exactly what we'd set out to do. We were building something with a foundation strong enough to scale. Even though people were just beginning to notice, the truth is, the most important work had already been done long before they were paying attention.

Process, Culture, and the Power of Curbs

I've never believed you can scale a business by sheer willpower. That works for a while, especially when you're hands-on, running one location, making decisions on the fly, but it only takes you so far. Eventually, if you want to grow something that lasts, you need more than energy. You need process. And not just any process. You need process that can flex without breaking.

> If you want to grow something that lasts, you need more than energy. You need process. And not just any process. You need process that can flex without breaking.

When people talk about process, they usually picture binders and rules, training manuals, and bureaucracy. But that's not what we built. From the beginning, I knew we needed something different, something that could create consistency without killing entrepreneurship. That balance became one of the defining tensions of our culture: How do you scale a business without turning your best people into box-checkers?

The answer, for us, became what we called *operating within the curbs.* It was a phrase we used all the time. Think of a city street. You're free to drive however you need to within your lane, but you've got to stay between the curbs. That was our model. Every dealership, every manager, had the autonomy to operate in a way that fit their market, their team, their style—as long as they stayed within the boundaries of what we considered nonnegotiable.

Those nonnegotiables were crystal clear: customer satisfaction, employee treatment, market share, and profitability. Those were the standards. Hit them, and you earned more leeway. Struggle with them, and the curbs narrowed. That's how we balanced structure with freedom. We didn't lead with policy but with performance.

But performance doesn't happen in a vacuum. You've got to communicate expectations clearly and often. I held town halls constantly, not just with executives, but with every level of the organization. When we bought a new store, I showed up on day one to walk through our Creed Card. I'd explain who we were, what we believed, and what we expected. I didn't delegate that message. I delivered it personally because culture can't be handed off like a memo.

Still, once that message is out, it has to cascade. That's where a lot of organizations fall apart. You say something in the boardroom, and by the time it reaches the front line, it's been diluted, reshaped, or lost entirely. I used to illustrate this with the old telephone game. You start with one sentence at the top, and by the time it's passed through a room of fifty smart, well-intentioned people, the last version barely resembles the original. It's not because people are trying to mess it up. It's just how communication works. If you want alignment, you have to overcommunicate. And you have to *inspect* what you *expect*.

That's a phrase we used constantly. If we said that employee satisfaction was a core value, then we measured it. We surveyed, we tracked turnover, we asked questions. To ensure a positive customer experience, we then followed the data, visited stores, read reviews, and watched behavior. Every auto manufacturer has a system they deploy to measure customer satisfaction; however, for a dealership to truly be successful long-term, you need to embrace the core values and processes that truly make a customer happy or even excited to do business with your dealership. We often discussed not "chasing a score," meaning not trying to simply score well on the reports we got each month from the OEMs, but truly embracing what it means to take care of our customers.

We also created intentional feedback loops. Every quarter, we brought general managers and financial partners together across the company to share what was working. No PowerPoint contests, no politics. Just real examples. Here's something we tried. Here's the result. If it worked in Lubbock, maybe it works in Santa Fe. Some of our best ideas came from the service lane or the reception desk and not necessarily from our senior leaders. We encouraged and celebrated that. We even built incentive programs around it.

What I learned quickly, though, was that top-down mandates rarely work. The bigger we got, the more tempting it was to send out company-wide directives—tighten inventory here, cut advertising there. Sometimes, that made sense in theory. But what we found was that one-size-fits-all policies almost never produced one-size-fits-all results. This means that in some operations, you may need to carry a larger inventory of a certain type of product while the same brand of dealership that sells to a different customer base may not be required to carry as much inventory. It was important for us to stay flexible on a location-by-location basis. A plan that worked perfectly in a metro dealership could be a disaster in a rural one. Trying to force uniformity usually created more confusion than clarity.

> One-size-fits-all policies almost never produced one-size-fits-all results.

Take inventory management. We once rolled out a company-wide target on days' supply (this is an industry term that is used to measure the amount of inventory you keep on hand compared to your most recent sales history) to lower carrying costs during a rising-rate cycle. It looked great in a spreadsheet. But we hadn't factored in regional demand differences or the nuances of brand allocations. Some stores hit the target with no problem. Others were crippled by it. We ended up walking it back, rethinking how we approached those decisions, and most importantly, learning to listen better. The next time, we started with input instead of a directive.

That shift—from command and control to shared ownership—became foundational to our culture. As we grew, we had to trust our local leaders more, not less. We had to believe in the people we'd hired and give them the space to execute. That's not always easy when you're used to being in control. But it's necessary. Scale requires discipline, but it also requires trust.

The more we grew, the more I came to see process and culture as two sides of the same coin. You can't scale chaos. But you also can't scale a culture where everyone's afraid to think for themselves. So we built curbs. Clear enough to guide. Flexible enough to empower. And over time, those curbs became one of the most important tools we had, not to restrict our people, but to unleash them.

The Right People Make the Business Scalable

Most people assume capital is the biggest obstacle to scale. That once you have the money, everything else falls into place. But that's not what I found. Money was never the problem—not after we raised the first round, not once we'd proven the model. My equity partners were more than willing to fund growth as long as we delivered results. What actually slowed us down wasn't capital. It was people.

I used to say this at every town hall when we welcomed a new acquisition: "We don't have a capital problem. We have a people problem." And I didn't mean that in a negative way. I meant that the thing that kept us from doubling our size or moving even faster wasn't access to deals or funding—it was whether we had the right leaders ready to carry the vision forward.

Jim Collins put it simply in *Good to Great*: Get the right people on the bus.[1] That concept became one of our bedrock beliefs. But we took it further, as Collins prescribed. It wasn't just about getting them on the bus. It was about making sure they were in the right seat. Someone might have had the talent and the values, but if they were in a role that didn't fit their skills or aspirations, we'd never get their best.

We saw this play out over and over again. A great finance leader who turned out to be an even better operator. A service manager who thrived when given a chance to lead a whole store. There wasn't a rigid path or a template we followed. We paid attention to performance, but we also paid close attention to alignment. Did they believe in our vision? Did they live our values? Were they committed to our four pillars—employee satisfaction, customer satisfaction, market share, and profitability? That last one gets emphasized in a lot of companies, but for us, it was never the only one that mattered.

I made that clear when we looked at internal promotions. If someone was killing it financially but their employee satisfaction was low or their customer experience was slipping, we didn't promote them. That wasn't the kind of leadership we wanted. On the other hand, when someone consistently delivered across all four pillars, they earned more than recognition; they earned responsibility. That's how we scaled: by finding people who could not only run a department but protect and pass along the culture.

And when we had those people, we did everything we could to keep them growing. One of the advantages of being a multistore, mul-

---

1   Jim Collins, *Good to Great: Why Some Companies Make the Leap ... and Others Don't* (HarperBusiness, 2001).

timarket organization was that we could offer mobility. If someone was ready for the next step but the opportunity didn't exist in their current store, we looked for openings elsewhere. Maybe it was across town. Maybe it was across the country. Either way, if we had the right person, we wanted to find the right place for them to keep developing.

Sometimes that meant taking a risk. Moving someone from sales to service, or from one market to another. Sometimes it meant moving someone into a role they hadn't done before because we believed in their leadership more than their résumé. I believed you could teach skills. You couldn't teach belief. You couldn't teach hunger, or integrity, or how someone treated the people around them. That either came with the person, or it didn't.

We also kept the door open for *everyone*. Even when someone left the company, we celebrated them if they were leaving for the right reasons. If it were a better opportunity, or a move for their family, we never made it adversarial. We sent them off well. More often than you'd think, they came back. After a year or two in a different culture, many of them realized how rare ours was. And when they were ready, we found a place for them again.

For RFJ, it was about building a system that sustained itself. We were trying to scale a belief system more than a business, one where people weren't treated like a cost center but like the core asset they truly were. That belief ran through every part of our organization. It shaped how we interviewed, how we promoted, how we handled mistakes, how we dealt with exits, how we built succession plans.

Every time we opened a new store, made a new hire, or added a new market, we asked the same question: Who's going to carry this forward? Not just hit the numbers. Not just keep the lights on. But who's going to extend the culture? Who's going to embody what this company actually stands for?

Those were the people who made RFJ scalable. Without them, it was just a good idea with some money behind it. With them, it became a movement.

When the Playbook Doesn't Work

The hardest part about scaling is knowing when to throw parts of the playbook out.

In the early days, we tried to bring the same structure and discipline to every store. That's what scale is supposed to be about, right? Process. Consistency. Replication. And for the most part, it worked. Until it didn't.

One of the most expensive lessons I learned came from how we managed inventory. We knew carrying costs were rising; interest rates had been ticking up for months. At one point, we had $750 million in inventory across the company. When rates jumped just half a point, that translated to more than $3.7 million in additional annual interest expense. That was money leaving the business.

The instinct, of course, was to respond with a mandate: Cut inventory. We set targets, issued new limits, pushed hard from the top down. In theory, it was a logical move to reduce exposure, tighten capital, and preserve margin. But what we didn't fully account for was how different every store actually was. We had domestic brands, import brands, luxury lines, high-volume operations, and niche rooftops. Some stores had fast turn cycles and could get cars quickly. Others were waiting months because of OEM constraints. Geography played a role, too. Demand in West Texas didn't always look like demand in New Mexico or Idaho.

So our one-size-fits-all mandate? It didn't fit anywhere.

Instead of reducing cost, we disrupted the rhythm of stores that were actually performing well. We limited operators who had a handle on their markets and knew exactly what they needed on the lot. Worse, we sent a message that we didn't trust them to make the call. That created friction. Friction slows scale.

That's when we hit pause and reevaluated.

I went back to a lesson I've learned over and over again: Education beats mandates. If our general managers understood the financial risk, the actual cost of excess inventory in a rising-rate environment, they'd adjust. But they needed context. So, we walked them through it and broke down the math. We showed them how every half-point hike meant real dollars flowing out the door.

Then we shifted the conversation.

Instead of issuing fixed limits, we asked each store to evaluate its position based on brand dynamics, floor plan terms, and sales velocity. We created tools to help them calculate exposure and make smarter local decisions. And we held them accountable to their numbers *and* to their reasoning. If a store was carrying more inventory than the model suggested, they had to explain why. Sometimes they had a great reason. Sometimes they didn't. Either way, it led to better decisions.

That approach required more trust. It also required more humility. The top-down model can feel efficient, but when you're managing dozens of variables across dozens of locations, efficiency is rarely the same as effectiveness. What we needed was adaptability, and that came from empowering the people closest to the ground.

I used to remind my team: Just because a strategy worked yesterday doesn't mean it'll work tomorrow. Markets change. Interest rates rise. Customer behavior shifts. As a company grows, the complexity doesn't scale linearly; it compounds. That means your leadership has to grow, too.

I look back at that moment, when we threw out the blanket mandate, and see it as a turning point. It was the moment we moved from managing stores to developing leaders. We stopped dictating and started equipping. And as a result, our decisions got better. Our teams got sharper. Our outcomes improved.

Scaling, I've learned, isn't just about expansion but *evolution*. The same playbook that gets you from zero to ten stores won't get you from ten to fifty. And the faster you grow, the more important it becomes to lead with curiosity, not control.

The best leaders I worked with during that time weren't the ones who stuck rigidly to the model. They were the ones who asked the tough questions, listened, adjusted, and were willing to say: The playbook doesn't work here; let's build a better one together.

That's what real "overnight" success looks like.

TIMELESS TAKEAWAYS

1. Vision is not enough. You have to build the invisible before anyone believes in the visible. The most admired growth stories are built long before the headlines start. Infrastructure, capital strategy, legal foundation, and deal flow pipelines (all the unglamorous work) must be built before revenue ever hits the books. Success that looks fast is usually just the public payoff for years of quiet preparation.

2. Character raises capital before any company ever does. When you don't have assets or revenue, your track record, reputation, and values are your collateral. Investors may look at spreadsheets, but ultimately, they bet on people. Before you ask someone to believe in your business, make sure you've built a track record that speaks for itself.

3. You can't scale without structure, but too much structure suffocates performance. Building systems is essential, but those systems must allow room for autonomy and judgment. The operating-within-the-curbs model gave operators flexibility to lead locally while staying aligned with company-wide nonnegotiables. That balance of discipline and freedom fueled sustainable growth.

THE PARTNERSHIP COMMITMENT

*Coming together is a beginning, staying together
is progress, and working together is success.*

—HENRY FORD

You learn a lot about people when everything goes wrong.

It's easy to say you're aligned when business is booming. It's easy to talk about shared values when the metrics are strong, the markets are steady, and everyone's winning. But the real test of a partnership, whether it's with an employee, a leader, or a capital provider, comes on the hardest day. The one you never saw coming.

For me, that day came when three people were killed in one of our showrooms.

It was a weekday evening. I was at dinner with my wife when the call came in: A team of bounty hunters had attempted to take down a fugitive inside one of our stores. The situation had spiraled out of control, and gunfire had erupted in the middle of the showroom.

Three people lost their lives—two of them were bounty hunters, one was the fugitive. Fortunately, not one of our employees or customers was injured, but the emotional impact on our people was profound.

There is no playbook for something like that. No business school prepares you for it. But in that moment, everything we'd spent years building, from our culture to our leadership standards, was put to the test.

The first call I made, as I was driving to the dealership myself, was to our team on the ground. "Is everyone safe? Are our people OK?" The next call was to our head of HR. We started pulling together crisis support, grief counselors, communication protocols, and logistics for shutting down operations and securing the site. I didn't think about profits or PR in those tense moments. All I could focus on was our people.

The next call I made was to our capital partner. When I explained what had happened, they had a simple response: "We're here for you. What do you need?"

There were no conditions, no questions about operational disruption, insurance coverage, or reputational risk. Just a simple, sincere offer of support. And in that moment, I realized something I had always believed but now understood at a much deeper level: The true value of a partner isn't what they offer when everything's going right. It's how they show up when everything goes wrong.

The true value of a partner isn't what they offer when everything's going right. It's how they show up when everything goes wrong.

Their response was quiet, steady, and fully aligned with how we wanted to lead through the situation. They didn't panic or micromanage. Instead, they asked the right questions: How are your people? What do you need from us? Are there any resources we can activate for you?

In the days that followed, we focused on our people and brought in counselors. We kept the store closed until we felt our team was ready. We communicated with transparency, both internally and externally. And we made sure that every decision we made reflected our values, not just our obligations. We didn't give a hoot about the optics. Our only concern was in doing what was right.

We also learned a hard truth about leadership: In a crisis, people don't just listen to what you say. They watch what you do. They pay attention to where you put your time, your resources, your concern. They remember whether you showed up or stayed silent. And in those moments, culture is either revealed or exposed.

> We also learned a hard truth about leadership: In a crisis, people don't just listen to what you say. They watch what you do.

In many ways, that day became a defining moment for our organization because of how we responded to a senseless tragedy. It reinforced everything we said we believed in and proved that those beliefs weren't just words on a wall. Our capital partner's response deepened our trust. It confirmed that we had chosen the right partner because of their character. They let *us* lead while offering support and backing every decision we made, even the ones that cost money.

There's a lesson here I want every founder to take seriously: You won't know the real strength of the relationship with your capital partner until you hit your worst day. That's when the promises are tested and alignment becomes either real or irrelevant.

The Partnership Is the Plan

The real world has never been kind to even the most meticulous business plans. No matter how well an operator builds their model, defines their vision, or sharpens their strategy, there will always be events that throw everything off course. These moments do not show up on a spreadsheet. They rarely follow logic. But they arrive all the same—often fast, always uninvited—and they test whether the structure you've built can hold under pressure. More importantly, they reveal whether the partner standing beside you has the character to weather the storm.

Over the course of my career, I've lived through more economic curveballs than I can count. We've briefly touched on some of these black swan events in an earlier chapter, but they bear repeating. In the early 1980s, interest rates climbed to levels that made financing almost impossible for the average consumer. I can still remember sitting in a showroom and watching people come in hoping to buy a car, only to realize the rates were in the mid-twenties on used vehicles. New car loans weren't much better. When you're facing 18 percent interest, the fundamentals of your business get rewritten. And the Gulf War rattled business confidence in ways that were hard to comprehend at the time.

Years later, the 2008 financial crisis hit the system with a different kind of force. I was at Sonic Automotive at the time, and while the company had the scale and resources to endure it, the industry as a whole was shaken to its core. I watched some of the most respected Wall Street firms collapse in real time. Bear Stearns and Lehman Brothers disappeared almost overnight. Even massive institutions such as J.P. Morgan had to be absorbed or propped up just to survive. That level of disruption hit every sector, including auto. For dealers, the shutdown of credit markets meant that floor plans disappeared. Without floor plan financing, a dealer can't carry inventory. And without inventory, they're out of business. At RFJ, there was a point when we were carrying roughly $750 million in vehicle inventory. No bank line meant that capital would have to come from somewhere else, and very few people can write a check of that size just to keep things moving.

But the single most disorienting event I experienced was the COVID-19 pandemic. It wasn't just a health crisis. For many businesses, it became a full-blown economic shock with uneven, unpredictable effects across regions and industries. For us, the impact was immediate. Certain states forced complete shutdowns of showroom floors, leaving us scrambling to understand what we were allowed to do and how quickly we could pivot. In some locations, even basic customer access was off-limits. We weren't permitted to sell cars in person. For a business built on face-to-face relationships and transactional momentum, that kind of restriction brought everything to a standstill.

In those first few days, we didn't wait around for clarification. I sat down with my team, and we built what I called the emergency plan. It wasn't elegant, and it wasn't theoretical. It was a series of detailed financial models that tracked how long we could survive at different revenue levels. We built scenarios for 75 percent of revenue, 50 percent, 25 percent, and even 0 percent. Every line item was scrutinized. We calculated the real burn rate, accounted for payroll obligations, and determined what levers we could pull to stretch our runway. The analysis was sobering, but it gave us a plan and a sense of control.

What provided us the confidence to move forward, even as the world felt like it was falling apart, was knowing we had a capital partner who was fully aligned. They didn't flinch. They didn't immediately ask about numbers or exposure. They asked how our people were doing and what support we needed. That kind of response can't be fabricated. It only comes from a relationship that has been built on trust and tested over time.

When founders talk about raising capital, they often focus on terms, valuation, and control. And those things do matter. However, I've come to believe that the most important element isn't the contract but the *character*. When the worst day arrives (and it always does in some form), you want someone on the other end of the phone who is calm, committed, and constructive. You want someone who sees the relationship as a shared journey, not a transactional obligation.

The truth is that most businesses will never experience only smooth sailing. That's not how the world works. There will always be disruptions, whether they come in the form of geopolitical conflict, interest rate volatility, collapsing financial systems, or a global pandemic. You can't predict the specifics, but you can build the right kind of foundation.

That foundation starts with partnership. It starts with asking hard questions before a deal is ever signed. Do we trust each other? Do we share the same long-term vision? Are we aligned on what matters most when the pressure is on? If the answers aren't clear, it doesn't matter how strong your business plan is. Because at some point, you won't be following it. You'll be rewriting it with your back against the wall.

> Don't just prepare your company for growth; prepare it for the unknown.

That's why I always tell entrepreneurs: Don't just prepare your company for growth; prepare it for the unknown. The right capital partner won't just believe in your vision during the pitch. They'll believe in your resilience when the plan breaks down.

And they'll help you build something strong enough to endure things you can't yet imagine.

For Better or for Worse

If you've ever been through the process of raising capital, you know the early conversations can feel a lot like dating. Everyone shows up dressed for the occasion with polished decks, practiced stories, curated charm. The energy is high, the smiles come easily, and there's a natural temptation to move fast. Especially when the checkbook is open. But what I've learned—what every founder eventually learns—is that raising capital isn't just a business transaction. It's a commitment. The person across the table isn't just writing a check; they're becoming a partner in your future. You wouldn't marry someone after a first date. And you shouldn't take on a capital partner that way either.

A strong capital relationship has to hold through uncertainty. It has to hold through tension. It has to hold through the days when no one's hitting their numbers and the answers are unclear. That's why I often compare choosing a partner to choosing a spouse. The vows you take in marriage—"for better or for worse, in sickness and in health"— are about more than ceremony. They're about staying aligned through everything you didn't plan for. Business is no different. The day you sign a deal with a capital partner, you're entering a relationship that will be tested. It's not a matter of if. It's a matter of when.

That's why alignment has to come first. Not terms. Not valuation. Not the size of the check. *Alignment.* You need to understand how they think about problems. What they value. How they behave under pressure. Are they calm in a crisis? Do they support or second-guess? Can you have a hard conversation without losing trust? These questions lay the grounded truth of whether a partnership is going to work when the terrain gets rough.

In my case, I was lucky. I didn't just end up with a well-capitalized firm. I ended up with a partner whose values and temperament matched my own. When we hit the biggest challenges of our journey, they listened and stepped in with the right questions, trusting us to lead the response. That kind of relationship has to be earned on both sides.

Too many entrepreneurs treat capital as a commodity. They assume that money is money, and whoever brings the best valuation is the right choice. But capital, in the wrong hands, becomes a liability. It adds friction where there should be trust and introduces second-guessing where there should be clarity. And it starts to distort decisions that should be made with a long-term lens. A partner who doesn't align with your values will eventually pull the business in a direction that no longer reflects your vision. It might not happen on day one. But it will happen, especially when things get hard.

There are a few simple signals I always encourage entrepreneurs to look for before committing to a capital partner. Do they give you references? And not just a couple of cherry-picked names, but a real list of current and former portfolio CEOs, people you can call and speak with directly. If they hesitate, that's a red flag. The best firms are proud of the relationships they've built and are eager for you to do your diligence. They want you to know who they are when the cameras aren't rolling

Another key test is whether they listen. Not just to your pitch, but to your perspective. Are they asking thoughtful questions about your business, your culture, your goals? Or are they trying to steer you toward their playbook before they understand yours? Listening is one of the most underrated skills in a capital partner. It shows respect and humility. And it tells you whether they see the relationship as a real partnership or just a transaction.

Timeline alignment is also critical. Some investors have a three- to five-year horizon. Others are long-term holders. Some are focused on growth at all costs, while others are centered on cash flow and asset value. None of these models are inherently wrong, but they can be wrong for *you* if they're not aligned with what you want to build. Don't assume an investor will adapt to your plan. Make sure your plan fits how they operate.

And finally, there's decision-making style. Every capital partner has one. Some want weekly check-ins. Some want autonomy. Some want to be involved in every inflection point. Others only step in during material events. Again, there's no universal right answer. But there's a right fit. The sooner you understand how a partner makes decisions, the sooner you'll know whether you're going to thrive—or clash—when the stakes are high.

A great capital partner does more than provide resources. They help you solve hard problems and build not just a bigger company but a more resilient one.

Choosing a partner is choosing the future of your business. So take the time, ask the hard questions, and look beyond the numbers. Because the person who writes your check might also be the one standing beside you when the entire business is on the line.

> Choosing a partner is choosing the future of your business.

Communication Builds the Relationship

In any meaningful partnership, communication is the backbone. It's essentially the operating system that either keeps things moving or lets the gears seize up. In my experience, what makes the difference isn't how often people talk, but *when, how,* and *why.*

When I think back to my years building RFJ, one of the most impactful routines I established had nothing to do with operations, acquisitions, or financial reporting. It was something we jokingly referred to as Good News Friday. Just about every other Friday, I would send a short email update to our equity partners. These weren't deep-dive reports or formal memos. They were personal, straightforward updates that simply said: Here's something great that happened this week. Maybe it was a new store acquisition. Maybe one of our dealerships hit a new sales milestone. Maybe we ranked first in a national brand metric. Whatever it was, I wanted them to know we were making progress.

At first, it seemed like a small gesture. But over time, I realized how much those updates mattered. They were reinforcing trust more than anything. They created a rhythm in our communication and set an expectation that we were going to stay connected, not just once a quarter, not just when the board packet went out, and not just when something was on fire.

That consistency built a level of visibility into our business that mattered a lot more than the numbers alone. When it came time for our board meetings, there were no surprises or uncomfortable pivots where someone asked, "Why are we just hearing about this now?" That's not the kind of relationship you want with a capital partner. If that's the dynamic you find yourself in, chances are the problem isn't the investor. It's *you.*

> Eventually, the truth comes out. And when it does, the issue won't just be the business; it'll be the trust.

Your partner can't support what they don't understand. And they can't understand what you don't tell them. That responsibility belongs to the CEO. As the founder or operator, you're the one closest to the business. If your instinct is to withhold, delay, or sugarcoat information, all you're doing is undermining the relationship. Eventually, the truth comes out. And when it does, the issue won't just be the business; it'll be the trust.

I've always believed that hard news is more important than good news. It tells your partner how much respect you have for them, how you lead under pressure. Above all else, it sets the tone for how the relationship will function when things get messy. I never waited for a quarterly review to share something material. If we were facing an issue, I picked up the phone. If a store was underperforming, if a manager needed to be replaced, if an external risk emerged, I didn't try to manage appearances. The only way to do that effectively is by bringing your partner into the conversation early.

There's a myth that transparency is just about being honest. That's part of it, but not the whole story. Real transparency is proactive communication: giving your partner the full picture so they can think with you, support you, and add value at the right time. That means being clear about what you know, what you don't know, and what you're trying to figure out. It also means admitting when you need help.

The mistake I've seen too many entrepreneurs make is assuming their job is to protect the investor from bad news. They think if they keep quiet long enough, they'll find a way to fix it and then share the cleaned-up version. But problems don't get smaller in the dark. They get more expensive. And the longer you wait, the less trust you'll have when you finally ask for support. If your partner has to dig for the truth, the relationship is already in trouble.

> But problems don't get smaller in the dark. They get more expensive.

At RFJ, our culture was built on open communication. That extended beyond our internal teams and right into our boardroom.

I wanted our partners to feel like they were part of the business, not outsiders looking in.

If there's one principle I would pass on to any founder considering outside capital, it's this: Communication doesn't end when the deal is signed. That's when it begins. Communication is what turns a funding event into a real partnership.

So, communicate often. Communicate clearly. Communicate honestly. And remember that your ability to lead your partner is just as important as your ability to lead your team. If they don't know how your business is performing, they can't help you succeed.

Partnership Means Confidence, Not Control

A capital partner can be the greatest accelerator of your business … or the greatest obstacle. That all depends on whether the relationship is built on control or on confidence.

When I think about what made our partnership at RFJ work so well, it wasn't that we never disagreed or we had every answer figured out from the beginning. What made the difference was how we interacted. My partners didn't try to run the business. They gave me the room to lead because they trusted I would bring them into the conversation when it mattered. I always did.

> A great capital partner isn't looking to control your business. They're looking for confidence that you can.

That balance matters more than people think. There's a misconception among some founders that once you take outside capital, you lose your autonomy. The board takes over, the partners want veto rights, and every decision feels like it needs to be cleared. I've seen that dynamic before, and I can tell you, once that tone sets in, it's hard to undo.

But here's the truth: A great capital partner isn't looking to control your business. They're looking for confidence that you can. And the way you build that confidence is by staying in front of the conversation. You don't wait until a deal is closed or a plan goes sideways. You communicate clearly, consistently, and directly. You tell them what you're doing and why. You invite their perspective, even when you don't agree. Especially when you don't agree.

Over time, that's what builds trust. And trust is what gives you the freedom to operate.

I remember vividly the first time we hit a real challenge that could have gone sideways fast. We were facing a downturn in a specific region—one of our larger stores had missed its projections, and the local economy was softening in ways we hadn't fully forecasted. There was a natural instinct to go into defensive mode. Cut costs. Pull back. Restructure. But that wasn't the answer. The better play was to double down on leadership, shift our marketing mix, and reposition the store's inventory to better match buyer demand.

I brought that strategy straight to our partners. I walked them through the situation, the plan, the rationale, and the risks. They listened and asked thoughtful questions. Then they said, "We back it." No interference or panic. Just support.

That kind of response happened because the foundation was already in place. The relationship was built on alignment, clarity, and mutual respect. A strong partner doesn't pretend to have all the answers. What they bring is experience, perspective, and pattern recognition. They've seen other businesses stumble, and they've seen what works. That makes them valuable sounding boards, but it doesn't make them your boss. *You're* still the one driving the business.

One of the biggest signs you've found the right partner is how they respond when you disagree. At RFJ, we didn't always see every issue the same way. That's natural. But we never let disagreement turn into dysfunction. We debated, challenged each other, and sometimes walked away from conversations with a decision that wasn't unanimous. And that was OK. What mattered was how those moments were handled: with respect and a shared commitment to the outcome.

In contrast, I've seen situations where entrepreneurs went with the wrong partner. The money might have been there, but the relationship was built on skepticism. Every board meeting felt like an interrogation. That dynamic can crush momentum and only creates a culture of defensiveness where founders hesitate to take smart risks because they're worried about explaining every step after the fact.

If that's how the partnership feels, the business won't scale. It might survive for a while, but it won't thrive.

So, before you take on a capital partner, ask yourself what kind of relationship you're signing up for. Are they investing in you because they believe in your leadership? Or are they investing because they want to run the business through you? Are they asking insightful questions, or dictating detailed solutions? Do they give you room to lead, or leave you constantly second-guessing your judgment?

These are the signals that matter. Because the truth is, you won't always get everything right. No founder does. But the confidence your partner has in you—and how it holds up when the winds shift—is what allows you to course-correct quickly, recover effectively, and keep building forward.

In the end, capital doesn't lead a company. People do.

TIMELESS TAKEAWAYS

1. The strength of your capital partner is revealed in your worst moments, not your best ones. Great partnerships aren't proven when the market is rising or when headlines are glowing. They're revealed when something goes wrong, when plans go sideways, or when a crisis hits without warning. In those moments, your partner either leans in with clarity and support or steps back with conditions and concerns. Whether you're facing a macroeconomic disruption, a personnel challenge, or an unexpected tragedy, what matters most is knowing your capital partner will stand beside you, not above you. The right partner doesn't flinch in adversity. They ask how they can help and trust you to lead through it.

2. Alignment isn't a slogan. It's the foundation … and it only gets more important over time. Shared values, mutual respect, and a long-term view are essential ingredients in any sustainable partnership. If you're not aligned on decision-making, communication cadence, and exit timelines at the start, those gaps will only widen under pressure. Alignment is what allows a founder to act quickly in a crisis without fear of second-guessing. It also sustains trust when circumstances shift, as they inevitably will.

3. Communication is the discipline that protects the relationship. You don't build trust by showing up quarterly with a polished presentation. You build it through frequent, honest, two-way communication, *especially* when the news is hard. Whether it's a missed forecast or an unfolding crisis, capital partners can only help if they understand what's happening in real time. Keeping your partners informed is essential to the health of the business. If you expect confidence from them, give them visibility.

CHAPTER EIGHT

IS IT TIME TO SELL?

From the very beginning, we built RFJ Auto Partners with a clear intention: to scale, grow, and ultimately sell. That decision shaped how we structured the company, how we managed our finances, and how we communicated our vision to investors. We didn't obsess over a specific revenue target or a perfect EBITDA multiple. What mattered was whether we had built something of lasting value, something large enough, stable enough, and attractive enough to be seen as a viable platform. Once we crossed that threshold, the timing of a sale became less about a milestone and more about maintaining awareness. Essentially, we were preparing for when the right partner arrived.

I've found that most founders assume there will be a clear moment when the For Sale sign goes up. But in practice, the moment rarely announces itself. Sometimes it shows up quietly, buried in a phone call from an investor who's heard about what you're building.

Other times, it comes in the form of a casual inquiry that ends up reshaping how you think about your business altogether. For RFJ, those moments started showing up earlier than even I expected.

Roughly two to three years after our founding, we began receiving serious inquiries. The first time it happened, I was a little surprised. We had been moving quickly—acquiring stores, building infrastructure, creating the backbone of a real business—but we were still relatively young. Yet here was a major public company from Japan reaching out, genuinely interested in making a move into US auto retail, and believing RFJ could be their entry point. That level of attention forced us to pause and consider where we stood. Were we ready? Could we entertain this sort of conversation seriously?

We decided to lean into the opportunity. I engaged in extensive conversations with the CEO of that company. In fact, we developed a real relationship. He was someone I came to respect deeply, and over time, our business talks evolved into a mutual admiration for each other's values and cultures. One of my favorite memories from that period is captured in a photo that still hangs on my wall. I had custom cowboy boots and a Texas-style hat made for the CEO, and he sent me a photo of himself standing proudly in his Tokyo office, wearing both and grinning from ear to ear. That picture reminds me of something that has stuck with me over the years: Even in deals that don't materialize, there's value in the relationship itself. Every conversation teaches you something. Every potential buyer helps you see your business through a different lens.

In the end, the timing wasn't right. Their team ultimately felt that RFJ was too large a bite for their first foray into the US market, and we mutually decided to part ways. But I walked away from that experience with sharper instincts, clearer documentation, and stronger conviction about what it would take to be ready when the next inquiry came.

And it did.

A few years later, a public company from Canada approached us with a similar intention: to expand into the US by acquiring a platform. Again, we opened the books, held discussions, explored alignment, and ultimately walked away. It wasn't a lack of interest. We just came to the conclusion that the fit wasn't there. Still, the process itself had real value. Each of these interactions forced us to reexamine how we presented our business, how we framed our story, and how we answered tough questions. They compelled us to stay ready, not just hopeful. As we matured, we came to appreciate these dialogues as strategic exercises in learning how others saw us.

My advice to other entrepreneurs is simple: Always take the call. Whether or not you think you're ready to sell, you gain something from every serious conversation about your business. You'll hear how others assess your strengths, where they believe your risks lie, and what stands out about your model from the outside. Sometimes those insights affirm your strategy. Sometimes they expose blind spots. Either way, they help you get better. If your goal is to build a valuable, enduring company, these moments are part of the work.

In hindsight, what helped RFJ the most was our willingness to treat every inquiry as if it could be the real thing. We didn't waste time chasing unlikely deals, but we never dismissed an opportunity to learn. We stayed curious and responsive. In doing so, we created the kind of operational readiness and reputational trust that made us attractive to the right buyer when the time came.

The clock on a sale doesn't start when you list the business. It starts the moment someone else starts paying attention to what you've built. That attention comes faster than most people expect. The real question is whether you're ready when it does.

You Can't Predict the Moment, but You Can Prepare for It

Long before a buyer made a serious offer to buy RFJ, we treated the company as if an audit could begin tomorrow. It wasn't a mindset driven by paranoia. It was a commitment to discipline. From day one, we maintained fully audited financials, managed through external firms, and held ourselves to public company standards even while operating as a private business. That standard kept us sharp. It meant that whenever a potential buyer came knocking, there would be no scramble to organize, no last-minute documentation, and no risk of surprises hidden in the details.

One of the most vivid examples of that philosophy in action came during the special purpose acquisition companies (SPACs) wave in the early 2020s. SPACs became a fast-moving trend, a vehicle for taking companies public through acquisition. Two separate SPACs approached us, both with serious interest in making RFJ their platform company. One of them progressed far enough that we reached an agreement on valuation and deal terms. But before the transaction could close, their financing structure fell apart. The capital markets shifted, and the window closed. On paper, it might have looked like a lost opportunity. In practice, it was another critical test of our preparedness.

During that process, our team learned just how much time and credibility can be saved when your house is already in order. The months spent in discussion validated the strength of our reporting, our systems, and our internal processes. The experience sharpened us, and when the right buyer finally arrived, those lessons allowed us to move with precision. Every conversation, every due diligence request, and every audit drill we had done in earlier years proved invaluable when it mattered most.

The foundation of that readiness rested heavily on the shoulders of one person: our CFO, Tamara Bebb. Tamara joined RFJ several years before our sale, and her impact on the business cannot be overstated. She brought with her a background in both public accounting and PE, experience that bridged two worlds that don't always communicate easily. She understood what investors look for, how auditors think, and what a buyer expects when evaluating a potential acquisition. Her commitment to precision changed the way we operated. Every report, every statement, and every audit cycle reflected a level of transparency that instilled confidence, internally and externally.

A great CFO doesn't just report numbers. They create the framework for trust. Tamara's discipline ensured that when the time came to share our financials with potential buyers, there were no inconsistencies or gaps that would force revaluation. Buyers could see exactly what they were acquiring, and that clarity built momentum. Deals fall apart most often when uncertainty enters the room. We never wanted uncertainty to be part of the conversation.

> A great CFO doesn't just report numbers. They create the framework for trust.

I've told many entrepreneurs over the years that one of the best investments you can make is in your finance leadership. A good

CFO can keep you compliant. A *great* CFO can prepare you for the moment when opportunity knocks. The difference is enormous. That level of preparedness doesn't just save time; it protects value. When your books are organized, when your documentation is current, and when your systems are aligned with professional standards, you control the narrative.

When Sonic Automotive ultimately approached us, that preparation became the decisive factor. Their president, Jeff Dyke, and I had known each other for many years. Our teams shared a mutual respect, and the cultural fit was strong. But even with trust and familiarity, no acquisition of that scale moves forward on good feelings alone. It requires data, verification, and evidence. Tamara's meticulous work meant that every number we presented held up to scrutiny. Every assumption was backed by documentation. That level of readiness allowed us to finalize valuation, complete diligence, and close the transaction in less than ninety days—a billion-dollar deal completed before year-end. In the world of corporate acquisitions, that timeline is extraordinary.

Preparation shortens distance and turns possibility into execution. The speed of that deal wasn't the result of luck or timing. It was the culmination of years of doing the small things right, over and over again.

The Right Fit Is Bigger than the Right Price

Every founder faces the moment when opportunity knocks, but the decision to sell a company goes deeper than a balance sheet. It touches something personal. Legacy, values, culture, and people—all of these matter just as much as valuation. In the case of RFJ, the most attractive offers were not always the ones with the biggest numbers. The offer that mattered most was the one that aligned with our vision and honored the people who had helped build it.

That belief was tested in full when a high-profile private investor approached us. This was someone with significant holdings across multiple industries—hospitality, entertainment, restaurants, and more. He was a well-known entrepreneur with a public profile, a track record of bold moves, and a genuine interest in expanding into the automotive space. His group already operated a small number of dealerships and had been watching RFJ's growth closely. His interest was serious, and conversations started quickly.

What made the approach especially compelling was the connection to one of his platform managers. That individual and I had worked together many years earlier, and we had kept in touch. The relationship helped bridge the initial conversation and gave both sides a level of comfort. The investor's team saw RFJ as a strong platform, and their ambition was clear. They wanted to go from one store to fifty, and they believed we were the vehicle to get them there.

From a financial standpoint, this buyer had the resources. From a capability standpoint, he had the infrastructure. But as those conversations unfolded, we began to assess the fit more deeply. We looked at how our cultures aligned, how decision-making would unfold, and how our team might integrate into a broader organization. These were the elements that would ultimately define the success of any merger. They would shape the future of our two thousand teammates, many of whom had grown with us from the early days.

As part of his due diligence, the investor reached out to Jeff Dyke, a longtime friend of mine and the president of Sonic Automotive. The two knew each other professionally, and Jeff was well positioned to offer insight into RFJ and my leadership. That phone call turned out to be more than a reference check. It created a bridge to what would become the final chapter in RFJ's independent story.

Soon after, Jeff called me directly. We had worked together before. I had spent part of my early career at Sonic, and many of the same executives who were there then were still in place. Fifteen years later, the leadership team remained intact, a testament to the kind of culture Sonic had built. That kind of continuity speaks volumes. People don't stay in roles that long unless the environment supports growth, values loyalty, and leads with integrity.

When Jeff and I began our discussion, it was about purpose more than price. We talked about what the combination of our two companies could mean for our teams. RFJ brought two thousand teammates to the table. Sonic had eight thousand. Together, we could offer broader career paths, greater opportunities for advancement, and access to deeper resources. It was a conversation built on shared values and long-standing trust, and it quickly became clear that this wasn't just another deal. It was the right fit.

The decision to sell to Sonic was rooted in the belief that leadership is about stewardship. From the beginning, my vision for RFJ was not just to build a business that performed well but to create something lasting. That meant taking care of our people, building a culture of accountability and trust, and preparing the company to thrive well beyond my tenure. The merger with Sonic fulfilled that vision. It allowed RFJ to continue growing within an organization that understood us, respected our way of operating, and valued the people who made it all possible.

Legacy isn't built on earnings alone. It's built on how you treat people, how you lead through transitions, and how you make decisions that reflect something larger than your own success. The Sonic deal brought that full circle. It validated the foundation we had built, the culture we had cultivated, and the relationships we had maintained. Most of all, it honored the promise I had made to myself and to my team—to build something enduring, something that would matter long after my name was no longer on the door.

The Perfect Exit Starts on Day One

You can't time the market, no matter how much you try. You can watch the headlines, track interest rates, listen to pundits, and even spot patterns. But you'll never know exactly when the environment will shift in your favor. What you can control is whether or not you're ready when it does.

Most people think of an exit as a destination. I've come to see it as a discipline. From the very beginning of RFJ, we built like the opportunity to exit could come at any moment. We didn't know exactly when or how, but we knew enough to respect the cycles. Timing might be uncertain, but preparation never has to be.

> Most people think of an exit as a destination. I've come to see it as a discipline.

In the business world, policy can change everything overnight. In our tire recycling company, we watched valuations climb rapidly when federal stimulus and environmental legislation suddenly spotlighted renewable energy. Trillions of dollars in spending were suddenly poured into clean tech and sustainability efforts. That tailwind elevated companies like ours almost instantly, not because we had changed anything, but because public attention and capital flowed into our sector. We believed in what we were building, but even we couldn't have predicted just how much valuations would rise in a matter of months.

No amount of analysis could have told us exactly when that wave would crest. But we were prepared to ride it when it did. That was the difference.

Across every business I've been involved in, from recycling to retail to real estate, I've carried the same mindset: Build from day one as if you might get the call tomorrow. That means your financials need to be clean. Your documentation needs to be consistent. Your people need to be ready. Your leadership team must be able to sit across the table from a potential buyer and answer the tough questions.

At RFJ, we implemented full audits from the very first year. The early results were messy. Those first reports didn't come back glowing, and that was the point. They showed us where we were vulnerable. They gave us a blueprint to improve. Over time, those annual audits became the backbone of our credibility. When the right buyer finally arrived, the diligence was a process we'd rehearsed for years.

Our deal with Sonic Automotive closed in just under ninety days. That pace is almost unheard of in a public-to-private transaction of that size. The reason it moved so quickly was muscle memory. It was the result of years spent preparing for a moment we couldn't predict.

Looking back, I'm grateful we didn't try to rush it. We had received acquisition offers years earlier, but we weren't ready. The market might have been warm, but our business needed more time in the oven. Exiting too early can shortchange everything you've worked to build.

That's why I believe the best exits are earned long before they happen. You don't get to control the moment. You only get to control the mirror you hold up to your business when that moment arrives. What will a buyer see? Will they see chaos or clarity? Will they see a leader who's buttoned up, or one still scrambling to get numbers in order?

In the end, the perfect exit wasn't perfect because the market cooperated. It worked because we were ready when it did. If there's one message I want to leave in this chapter, it's this: Build every day like the opportunity could arrive tomorrow. The right moment doesn't announce itself. It simply rewards those who are ready.

TIMELESS TAKEAWAYS

1. Your exit clock starts earlier than you think. Most founders imagine an exit as a decision they'll make someday. But in reality, the groundwork for that moment is laid in the early days, sometimes before the first dollar is raised or the first customer walks through the door. Every clean financial report, every leadership hire, every process you document becomes part of the foundation that makes a successful exit possible.

2. Being prepared is more valuable than trying to predict. No one can time the market, not in the stock market and not in business. Public policy shifts, interest rates change, and capital trends move quickly and often without warning. But preparation means discipline. When your books are audit-ready, your team is aligned, and your strategy is well-documented, you give yourself the flexibility to move fast when opportunity knocks.

3. The right buyer sees more than your numbers. Buyers aren't just investing in a business; they're stepping into its culture, people, and future. Fit matters. Shared values matter. When the right partner shows up, the goal is to build a relationship strong enough to carry both sides through the transition.

CHAPTER NINE

THE JOURNEY FROM CEO TO EMPLOYEE

Legacy is not leaving something for people. It's leaving something in people.

—PETER STROPLE

When most people think about selling a company, they imagine it as a finish line. But in truth, it's more like a relay exchange, one that requires precision, trust, and a period of overlap before the baton can be fully handed off. If your company is worth acquiring, it's because the people who built it brought something distinctive to the table. That includes *you*. And that's exactly why most acquirers will ask the founder or CEO to remain in place for a transition period.

In my case, that transition was a two-year commitment to stay on and help lead RFJ into its next chapter as part of Sonic Automotive. They didn't ask me to stay because of a contractual formality but rather because what we'd built at RFJ was operating with its own systems, processes, and culture. Folding that into a much larger organization required thoughtful, deliberate integration.

I've seen transition arrangements last anywhere from sixty days to three or more years, depending on the size of the business and the degree of operational difference between the buyer and the seller. For us, it was clear that we were coming in with a distinct operating model. Sonic understood that. They wanted to learn how we drove our customer satisfaction numbers, how we built our culture, and how we executed with consistency across markets. More importantly, they wanted to preserve what was working, not just absorb it.

That kind of continuity protects momentum. For employees, leadership visibility is critical in the wake of a sale. Uncertainty creates fear, and fear creates turnover. If the person who built the company disappears overnight, people start to assume the worst. They worry about their jobs, their roles, and their place in a structure that suddenly feels foreign. But if they see the same leaders still showing up invested and engaged, they're more likely to stick around and believe in the road ahead.

The same goes for performance. Maintaining your business's rhythm during integration is no small feat. The transition period means translating all the knowledge, systems, and infrastructure from one business to another without losing your stride. In our case, that meant mapping every corner of our operations onto a new corporate framework.

We had to rethink everything from payroll and benefits to inventory tracking and accounting. I distinctly remember standing in a room with my team, staring at what looked like an endless checklist. We cataloged each major system, policy, and process that needed to be merged or replaced. It was technical, methodical, and sometimes overwhelming work. But it was essential.

At the top of that list was payroll. It may sound obvious, but getting people paid accurately and on time is one of the most fundamental responsibilities any business has. We had been using one system while Sonic used another. And if we didn't manage the transition with care, we risked disrupting the very thing that keeps people showing up. So, we prioritized it, dedicated resources to it, and made sure we could answer every what-if scenario before pulling the trigger.

Next came HR and benefits. People don't always realize just how intricate that kind of integration can be. You're talking about transitioning thousands of employees across health plans, retirement systems, and compliance structures. That takes months of planning. And unlike some operational changes that can be phased in, HR systems have hard cutoffs. You can't afford to get it wrong.

The same was true for inventory systems, accounting platforms, and operational procedures. Each department had its own set of tools, reports, and routines. All of it had to be aligned. And because Sonic was a public company, there were strict timelines and reporting requirements we had to meet. Our standards were already high, but theirs were higher. That shift demanded not only process changes but a cultural reset around accountability and documentation.

That's why we approached integration like a project in its own right. We didn't just blend into Sonic; we built a playbook, taking the time to identify the critical points of connection and mapping out what needed to change, what needed to stay, and what needed to evolve. We created a road map that allowed us to sequence the work over twelve to eighteen months without derailing our day-to-day operations.

Looking back, I realize just how much those two years mattered. They were a continuation of leadership, just in a different context. And they gave us the opportunity to protect what we'd built while helping Sonic see the value they had acquired beyond our stores: in our people, our systems, and the principles that held it all together.

Leadership Without the Final Say

For most of my professional life, I'd operated with a clear sense of autonomy. As CEO, I didn't just guide the ship; I decided where it was headed. Every major decision, every final call, every tough judgment ultimately landed at my desk. That's what leadership meant to me. However, when you sell your company and step into an employee role, even if it's a senior one, the equation changes. Learning to lead within a different structure requires intentional adaptation.

> Learning to lead within a different structure requires intentional adaptation.

After the sale to Sonic Automotive, I agreed to stay on and continue leading operations through a two-year transition. On paper, many of my responsibilities remained the same. I still oversaw performance, led teams, and made key operational decisions. But what had changed was the chain of authority. I now reported to *someone else*. No matter how much mutual trust and history we shared, the reality was simple: I no longer had the final say.

That's a bigger shift than most people realize. You can't just walk into a new organizational chart and expect everything to feel the same. Even with the best relationships, the dynamics change. You move from being the owner and ultimate decision-maker to becoming a key contributor within someone else's system. The sooner you come to terms with that, the smoother your transition will be.

I was fortunate, however. The leaders at Sonic—specifically Jeff Dyke and David Smith—were people I had known for many years. I respected them deeply, and they gave me a great deal of latitude to continue running RFJ with the autonomy I had earned. But there were still boundaries. There were still approvals to get, budgets to align, and strategic decisions that required consensus. That's the nature of working inside a larger organization, especially one with public accountability.

One of the most important things I did in those early months was get crystal clear on the expectations. I asked the same questions I had always expected my own people to ask me: Who do I report to? What do they need from me? What are the limits of my authority? Where am I expected to lead independently, and where am I expected to collaborate or escalate?

I've always believed that clarity is a gift. As a CEO, I tried to provide it. Now, I had to seek it. I didn't want to assume anything. I wanted to understand exactly how to operate in this new structure. And the truth is, most frustrations in a transition such as this come from a lack of alignment around expectations. You think you're empowered to make a decision, but you're not. Or you hesitate to act, when in fact, you were the right person to move something forward. That's why asking questions up front matters so much.

What also shifted was the lens through which decisions had to be evaluated. At RFJ, I focused on what was best for our two thousand employees and our portfolio of dealerships. That was my universe. But once we became part of Sonic, the universe expanded dramatically. We were now part of a company with more than ten thousand employees. Every decision we made—whether it involved benefits, systems, inventory, or personnel—had ripple effects across a much broader landscape.

That's where mindset matters. You can't approach integration from a siloed perspective. You have to zoom out, align with broader goals, and understand that the strength of the organization depends on shared direction. In many ways, it mirrors what I used to tell my own leadership team: Leadership doesn't always mean having the last word. It means being accountable for the right outcome, even when you're not the one who makes the final call.

> Leadership doesn't always mean having the last word. It means being accountable for the right outcome, even when you're not the one who makes the final call.

This chapter of my career reminded me how important it is to lead with clarity, humility, and a strong sense of purpose. It's easy to lead when you control everything. It's harder (and in many ways more rewarding) to lead within a system where collaboration, communication, and trust determine your impact.

The truth is, leadership without the final say isn't lesser. It's just different. It calls for a different kind of influence, one rooted in credibility, alignment, and the ability to add value within a shared structure. For any founder moving into a post-sale role, embracing that shift is the key to making the most of the opportunity ahead.

When you sell the company you built, the deal doesn't end with a wire transfer. The more meaningful part often begins after the transaction closes, when you and your team are absorbed into a larger culture and the reality of integration begins to unfold. For me, stepping back into Sonic Automotive as an employee brought a level of professional reflection I hadn't expected. Years earlier, I had contributed to Sonic's early DNA. Now, I was reentering the company but in a different capacity, walking back into a culture I knew well, though from a different vantage point.

Life After the Deal—What Comes Next

Exiting a business doesn't mean exiting your purpose. For many founders, the close of a deal is just the start of a new kind of journey, one that's less about driving enterprise value and more about building a broader, more personal legacy. That was certainly the case for me.

When I transitioned out of RFJ, I didn't want to just drift into whatever came next. I took intentional steps to map out what this next season would

> Exiting a business doesn't mean exiting your purpose.

look like. It started with a commitment to my wife: We would travel more. Not just travel, but have uninterrupted time together. During my four decades of being tied to a demanding schedule, vacations were often limited to ten days at best, and even those were never truly disconnected. Stepping away from day-to-day operations meant I could finally prioritize quality time without constantly checking in or putting out fires.

That decision to slow down, even briefly, wasn't made in a vacuum. I took inspiration from my longtime friend and mentor Mike Maroone, who spent two decades helping build AutoNation after selling his own dealership group. When he finally stepped away, Mike did something profound: He gave himself an entire year off before committing to anything new. He used that time to reflect, recharge, and ask deeper questions about what he wanted his next chapter to mean. That stuck with me. So when my two-year transition with Sonic ended, I gave myself room to do the same.

That space led me to something I had already begun preparing for during my transition: our family office. Even as I wrapped up my responsibilities with Sonic, I was quietly building the foundation for this new venture. I wasn't doing it alone. From the beginning, the goal was to involve my children in a meaningful way. All three have taken active roles, and it's been one of the most fulfilling parts of my life to see them step into those responsibilities with vision and commitment.

Each of my sons has launched and scaled their own businesses in adjacent industries. My oldest owns and operates a tractor and powersports dealership, and we're already exploring opportunities for expansion. My middle child has acquired three powersports dealerships with a fourth on the way. These ventures allow them to operate in a space similar to where I spent most of my career, without ever directly competing with Sonic. That was important to me. I've always believed loyalty matters, and I wouldn't feel right going head-to-head with the people who trusted me enough to carry forward what we had built together.

My daughter, too, has been an important part of the family office. After starting her career in banking, she came onboard and quickly became a trusted contributor. Her path took an unexpected turn with the arrival of our fourth grandchild—a joyful surprise that brought new meaning and new complexity to her professional life. I've watched her navigate the dual demands of motherhood and leadership with grace, and I'm excited to see how her role evolves as she balances both over time.

Watching my children grow into these roles has reshaped my sense of what legacy really means. It's not about holding on to control or recreating what was. It's about passing on knowledge, values, and opportunity in a way that equips the next generation to lead on their own terms. That's where the real fulfillment lies: empowering others to grow into leaders themselves.

At this point in my life, I still have the drive to contribute, but the ways I contribute have changed. Mentorship has become a central part of that. I find purpose in advising other entrepreneurs, helping them think strategically about growth, culture, and exit planning. I enjoy sitting with them as they work through tough questions, because I've lived those same questions. I know what it means to pour everything into a company, to wonder what's next, and to wrestle with the weight of transition. If I can offer clarity or encouragement in those moments, that's a worthwhile way to spend my time.

The truth is, building a company was never just about financial success for me. It was about creating something lasting that helped people, created careers, and set others up to achieve more than they thought possible. That hasn't changed. I may not be running dealerships anymore, but I'm still in the business of helping people find their path.

This next chapter is about doing that on a broader scale. Whether it's through the family office, through my children's businesses, or through a conversation with a founder looking for direction, I still wake up with purpose. The form is different, but the mission remains the same: Help others grow, give back what I've learned, and keep building something that matters.

TIMELESS TAKEAWAYS

1. A successful exit includes a thoughtful transition because founders aren't just selling a business; they're handing over a culture, a team, and years of embedded leadership. Staying on during a post-sale transition provides employees with needed stability and gives the new owner access to critical institutional knowledge. Whether that commitment is sixty days or two years, it should be intentional, clearly defined, and rooted in shared goals.

2. Redefining leadership requires clarity and humility. When you're no longer the final decision-maker, success depends on understanding your new role, communicating expectations, and operating with respect for the new structure. Founders who embrace this shift with openness rather than resistance position themselves to stay productive, collaborative, and fulfilled in their new capacity.

3. Life after the deal deserves just as much planning. Exiting doesn't mean stepping away from purpose; it means stepping into a new kind of legacy. Whether through mentoring, launching a family office, or helping the next generation rise, the transition is most fulfilling when it reflects your values, priorities, and long-term vision.

CHAPTER TEN

CREATING A LEGACY

When I first set out to build RFJ, I didn't know exactly how far the road would take us, but I knew the direction. I wanted to build something that would outlast me. A company that stood for something. A company that meant something to the people inside of it, and perhaps even to the broader industry. The idea of legacy for me wasn't my name on a building. It was building an organization that could thrive, adapt, and evolve well beyond my tenure.

I often thought about Ford Motor Company when I imagined what RFJ could become. Ford didn't start with the goal of becoming a hundred-year company, and yet, that's what it became—multigenerational, enduring, still largely guided by the values of its founding family. That was the vision I carried.

Now, in our case, I always knew an exit would eventually come. We had an equity partner from the start, which meant RFJ was never designed to remain privately owned by me alone for the long haul. That's the nature of bringing on capital partners; they have investment horizons, and eventually, those timeframes converge with major decisions. However, just because an exit is inevitable doesn't mean your influence ends. An exit event doesn't have to mean the end of your legacy. That distinction is critically important for any founder to understand.

There's a common misconception that if you sell your company, you're walking away from everything you've built. In my experience, that's just not true. What matters far more than the structure of the deal is who you're handing the business to. In many ways, finding the right buyer is like hiring your successor. You want someone who sees what you've built and believes in its value beyond the numbers: the people, the culture, and the purpose that holds it all together.

What I tell any founder with an equity partner is to be ready, but don't rush. Stay open to the idea that your company might have more than one phase of equity sponsorship. It's common to have more than one capital partner over time, with each phase bringing new resources and opportunities for growth. What matters most is that each partner fits where the company is at the time and where it needs to go next.

In our case, Sonic Automotive proved to be that fit. I've said it before, but it bears repeating because it defined the decision: We weren't just looking for a financial transaction; we were looking for alignment. The people at Sonic understood what we had built at RFJ.

They valued the same things. *Culture* was not a corporate buzzword to them any more than it was to us.

The RFJ story didn't end at acquisition, but instead it entered a new chapter, one that still carries the DNA of the company we built from the ground up. And that's what legacy really is.

Building a Family Office with Purpose

For some, an exit means winding down. But for me, it was the beginning of another kind of work: just as meaningful, but shaped by a different sense of purpose. I had spent a lifetime in a business that demanded everything I had. So the idea of simply retiring and stepping back didn't appeal to me. I wanted to build something that allowed me to remain engaged while creating opportunities for the people I care most deeply about—my family.

That's where the vision for Ford Family Investments began to take shape. I saw it as more than a holding company or an investment vehicle. I saw it as a new platform, one that could serve our family for generations. The structure had to be sound, but the heart behind it mattered just as much. I wanted it to reflect our values. I wanted it to foster a culture of involvement, responsibility, and stewardship. And I wanted it to give my children the opportunity to step into leadership in their own way, on their own terms.

All three of my kids had shown an interest in being involved. Two had worked with me at RFJ prior to the sale, and the third was just getting started in her own professional journey. Each brought a different skill set and perspective, which made the opportunity to work together even more meaningful. The family office created a shared space where we could collaborate, learn from one another, and stay aligned in our values while pursuing different interests.

From the start, I wanted Ford Family Investments to be more than just a place where we managed assets. It needed to be intentional in both structure and purpose. We built the office around three investment pillars, each designed to reflect a different strategy for long-term growth, stewardship, and involvement.

The first pillar focuses on income-producing real estate. These are long-term holds, often structured as triple net leases, designed to provide stable, recurring income. I like to call them our "boring mailbox money" investments. They aren't flashy, and they don't make headlines, but they offer durability. The assets are tangible. They serve as a steady financial foundation, one that is simple to manage and provides consistency across market cycles.

The second pillar involves fund-based investments. We participate as limited partners in several PE and VC funds, and I also serve on a few advisory boards. This approach allows us to stay active in the investment community, benefit from professional deal flow, and support strong managers without shouldering the operational burden. It's a way for us to remain intellectually engaged in the world of business and finance while building connections that can lead to future opportunities.

The third pillar, and arguably the most meaningful for me, is direct investment in operating companies. These are businesses in which we take a significant equity position and engage directly with the management teams. In some cases, I sit on the board or serve as a strategic advisor to the CEO. In others, we partner alongside founders and help them scale. This pillar is about backing the right people—entrepreneurs who are driven, mission-aligned, and in need of support to get to the next level. Many of these relationships started years ago. They've grown through mutual trust and shared values, and they represent the kind of mentorship that brings real satisfaction.

Each of these pillars serves a purpose. Together, they form a structure that supports long-term stability while leaving room for growth and evolution. More importantly, they give our family a way to stay grounded in the principles that guided RFJ: **clarity**, **culture**, **commitment**, and **care for people**. We built this office not just to preserve wealth, but to create opportunity. That's what legacy looks like when it's done with intention. It becomes less about control and more about continuation. Less about personal gain, and more about helping the next generation carry forward the values that built everything in the first place.

Ford Family Investments is still young in the grand scheme of things, but the foundation is solid. It reflects the journey we've been on and the values we want to see endure. It's a living continuation of the work I've always loved: supporting people, growing businesses, and building something that matters.

Investing in People, Not Just Companies

Over the years, I've looked at hundreds—maybe thousands—of investment opportunities. Some came packaged with flashy numbers and slick decks. Others arrived more humbly, through a conversation or an introduction from someone I trust. And if there's one thing I've learned, it's this: The real investment isn't in the product, the business model, or the market opportunity. It's in the person leading the company.

My approach has always been to invest in the jockey, not just the horse. I want to back people who are resilient, mission-driven, and emotionally committed to what they're building. That's true whether they're just getting started with an idea on paper or they've been in business for twenty years. What matters most is the substance of the person behind the company. Do they know their people? Do they care about culture? Are they clear on their purpose? Those are the questions that help me decide whether I want to get involved.

I've been fortunate to work with a number of entrepreneurs over the years who embody those qualities. One example is a young leader I've mentored for over a decade who's now building a roll-up strategy in the powersports and tractor space. Another is a former vendor from my RFJ days who launched his own software company and came to me for advice. In both cases, I wasn't drawn in by the industry or the numbers alone. I believed in them as people. I saw their work ethic, their values, and the way they treated others. That's what moved me to get involved, and that's what continues to guide my decisions today.

When I evaluate a potential deal, I always ask founders to tell me about their team. I want to hear the stories. Who helped them get started? Who's been by their side through the hard moments? What kind of culture have they created, and how do they support their people? If a founder can't answer those questions—or worse, doesn't seem interested in answering them—it usually tells me everything I need to know. The numbers might be impressive. The growth projections might look great on paper. But without that human element, I'm not interested. Because for me, business is personal.

The companies that last are built by people who care deeply, not just about the product or the profits, but about the people who help them get there. That mindset extends to how they build their leadership teams. One of the most critical hires any founder can make is their CFO. Yet, too often, I see leaders treat that role as a back-office function rather than a strategic partnership. A great CFO isn't just someone who manages the books. They're a partner who helps shape the financial architecture of the business, manage risk, and make sound long-term decisions.

At RFJ, I was incredibly lucky to have Tamara, our CFO mentioned earlier, who played that kind of role. She was a true business partner, and we wouldn't have reached the level of success we did without her. That experience reinforced how vital it is to invest in the right people throughout the entire organization. I've carried that lesson forward into every company I touch through the family office. When I see a CEO who's invested in finding and empowering the right CFO, it tells me they understand what it takes to build something that lasts.

I don't invest in every deal that crosses my desk. In fact, I pass on far more than I accept. For the handful I do pursue, the decision always starts with a belief in the person. I need to see passion, clarity of purpose, and a deep respect for people. If those aren't present, no amount of potential upside can change my mind. Because the legacy I want to leave behind isn't about how many zeros are in the bank account. It's about the people I've helped along the way. The entrepreneurs who went on to build great businesses, the teams who thrived under strong leadership, and the lives that were better for having been part of something meaningful.

That's what investing is really about. And for me, that's where legacy begins.

Legacy Beyond the Balance Sheet

When people hear the word *legacy*, they often picture a name on a building, a headline-grabbing valuation, or a transaction that sets financial records. And while those things are fine markers of a journey well traveled, they don't come close to how I define legacy. For me, legacy has always been about people. It's about the lives you touch, the opportunities you create, and the belief you pass on to others that they can do more than they ever thought possible.

Looking back, the moments that stand out to me are tied to the people I've had the chance to help. I've seen firsthand what happens when you give someone a stake in their own future—when you open the door for them to become an owner, not just an employee. In many of our investments through the family office, we've structured deals that provide operators with a real equity path. Sometimes we've financed their buy-in; other times we've walked alongside them as they grew into the role of full ownership. Those are the deals that mean the most to me. Because in those cases, the success doesn't end with me … it continues on through *them*.

Two of my own children are now business owners themselves. They're partners in ventures where we've taken a minority position and allowed them to lead. Watching them build something of their own, take risks, make decisions, and earn the trust of their teams—that's the kind of pride no sale price could match. And beyond my own family, I've had the privilege of working with operators in industries ranging from tire recycling to software, each of whom I believed in enough to help fund and mentor. In every one of those cases, the return I value most is seeing someone create generational change for their own family.

If I could speak to a younger version of myself, the first word I'd offer is patience. I spent a lot of my early years trying to force things to happen on my own timeline. What I came to understand is that patience doesn't mean slowing down but rather knowing when to push and when to prepare. I'd also tell that younger version of myself to focus less on control and more on contribution. You don't need to be the loudest voice in the room. You just need to be consistent, reliable, and anchored in purpose.

Entrepreneurship often gets glamorized. People see the upside and the freedom and assume it's all about prestige. What they don't see are the nights spent wondering if you'll make payroll, the weight of knowing that dozens or even hundreds of families are counting on your judgment. That's the part of entrepreneurship that's harder to describe but far more defining.

> You don't need to be the loudest voice in the room. You just need to be consistent, reliable, and anchored in purpose.

The most fulfilling part of this chapter in my life is knowing that the work continues, just in new ways. Through Ford Family Investments, I get to keep mentoring, keep investing, and keep building. But I also get to step back when it's time and let others take the lead. That's part of legacy, too. It grows when you release it. When you pass forward your knowledge, your resources, and your belief in someone else's potential.

I've often said that RFJ's legacy didn't end with its sale to Sonic. It just took on a new shape. The same is true of my own. Whatever I've built, whatever success I've had, means more when it becomes a stepping stone for someone else. That's the legacy I'm proudest of. And that's the one I'll keep building, one person at a time.

TIMELESS TAKEAWAYS

1. Legacy is built through people, not permanence. A lasting impact requires intentional investment in others. When you help someone rise higher than they believed they could, you leave behind something that endures far beyond any title or transaction.

2. The next chapter deserves just as much vision as the first. Exiting a company doesn't mean stepping away from purpose. Whether it's a family office, mentorship, or new ventures, your second act can be just as meaningful when it's built around your core values and designed for contribution.

3. Stewardship multiplies when it's shared. Empowering others with ownership—whether your children, partners, or protégés—creates a ripple effect. True legacy grows when you invite others in, give them a stake, and walk with them as they build their own path forward.

CONCLUSION

One of the core truths I've come to believe over the course of my career is that capital is not scarce. There is money out there (plenty of it, in fact) looking for a good home in businesses that are built to last. The challenge for founders isn't whether capital exists. The challenge is being ready to receive it and being thoughtful enough to choose the *right partner* when that moment arrives.

Every chapter in this book has tried to reinforce that idea. A capital partner isn't a quick fix or a shortcut. It's not a finish line or a retirement plan. It's an accelerant. The right one can help you grow faster, go further, and build something stronger than you could have built on your own. But it only works if you are honest about what your business truly needs and you're intentional about whom you bring to the table. When you take the time to understand your own goals—how you want to grow, what you want to preserve, and where you hope to go—then you'll know what kind of capital partner you need.

That clarity is what gives you leverage. Without it, you risk partnering with someone who might fund your next chapter but undermine the values and vision that brought you this far in the first place.

Looking back, the best decisions I made with RFJ were the ones rooted in preparation. From the start, I knew we needed to build the company like we'd sell it tomorrow, even if we had no plans to do so anytime soon. That mindset changed how we operated. We kept clean books, ran annual external audits, and invested in leadership development across every level of the business. We documented everything: our capital structure, our decision-making processes, our succession plans. We treated culture as an operating system, not a slogan. We knew we couldn't predict when the right partner would come along, but we wanted to be ready if they did.

That preparation gave us the freedom to have real conversations when buyers came calling. Most importantly, it allowed us to be discerning. We could wait for the right fit. And when that fit finally showed up, we could move quickly because we had already done the hard work. That was a deliberate decision we made long before we ever considered selling.

If you've read this far, I hope that's the message you'll carry with you. Capital is absolutely within reach. The partners are out there. What matters most is whether your business and your mindset are truly prepared for what that partnership requires. That begins with clarity and is sustained by discipline. And in the end, it is rewarded through alignment.

You only get one chance to choose the right partner. Take your time and ask the hard questions. Then listen closely to the answers. And above all, be honest about what you're building, whom you're building it for, and where you hope it can go. The right partner will not only understand that vision; they'll help you bring it to life.

The Responsibility of Success

After the RFJ sale, I found myself facing a different kind of challenge. I was no longer running a company with thousands of employees and hundreds of moving parts. For the first time in decades, I had the space to think about what success meant in the years ahead. That pause, brief as it was, gave me the perspective to ask an important question: Now that I had built something, how would I use it?

Ford Family Investments was born out of that question. I didn't create it just to stay busy or to find new ways to grow capital. I built it to serve as a platform for mentorship, partnership, and generational impact. It became a structure that allowed me to keep doing what I've always loved: helping people achieve more than they thought possible.

Throughout this book, I've talked about capital as a tool. That belief still holds true. Capital can unlock growth and solve complex problems. It can take a good business and help it become a great one. But for me, the most meaningful use of capital has always been the opportunity it creates for others. That includes the operators who now own a share of the companies they help run as well as the young entrepreneurs I've mentored who needed a first chance to prove them-selves. It also includes my own children, each of whom has chosen to step into the family office in their own way, learning not just how to invest, but how to lead.

When I think about success now, I think in terms of stewardship. I have been incredibly fortunate in my life, but I've never seen any of it as mine to hold forever. The real measure of success is whether it can be handed off and shared and whether it makes others stronger in the process. That's what drives the decisions we make at Ford Family Investments. We look at every opportunity through that lens. Does this build something lasting? Does it help someone else rise? Does it align with the values that have guided me from the beginning?

As I continue to partner with new founders and early-stage companies, I find myself repeating the same lessons I had to learn the hard way: Invest in your people. Choose your CFO wisely. Prepare your business like you'll sell it tomorrow. Define what you stand for before anyone else tries to define it for you. These are the principles that helped RFJ grow into something real, and they are the same principles I look for in the leaders I now support.

Legacy is not a plaque or a name on a building. It grows when it is passed forward and becomes stronger when it takes root in someone else's story. That is the responsibility of success: to create more of it, far beyond your own experience.

I have no interest in slowing down. The work just looks different now. The tools may have changed, but the purpose has not. Every meeting, every mentorship conversation, every investment decision is another chance to carry forward the lessons I've learned and to help someone else build something that matters.

An Invitation to Build Boldly

For founders thinking about the next chapter of their business—whether that means a capital raise, a strategic partner, or a future sale—the landscape is both exciting and challenging. Growth capital interest in founder-led businesses has only accelerated. The level of diligence, speed of execution, and complexity of deals continue to rise. Sophistication is no longer limited to buyers. It's expected from sellers, too.

That means preparation matters more than ever. Financials need to be clean, and leadership needs to be deep. And let's not forget that culture needs to be more than a slogan. This is the foundation that must already be in place long before the first serious conversation is ever had.

Whether you're just starting your journey or already preparing for a transition, I hope this book has helped clarify what's possible.

There's no single blueprint for success, but there are timeless principles that hold true across industries and market cycles. When you combine vision with discipline and leadership with the right kind of capital, you can build something that lasts.

If you are one of those leaders, I'd love to hear your story. At Ford Family Investments, we continue to look for opportunities to back bold entrepreneurs who are building for the long term. We look for fit, for shared values, and for partners who believe that capital is most powerful when it's used to create opportunity for others.

This is the work that matters.